ROOT OF ALL EVIL?

How to Make Spiritual Values Count

ANTONIA SWINSON

SAINT ANDREW PRESS
EDINBURGH

First published in 2003 by
SAINT ANDREW PRESS
121 George Street
Edinburgh EH2 4YN

ISBN 0 7152 0805 5

British Library Cataloguing in Publication Data
A catalogue record for this book is available from the British Library

Antonia Swinson's website is www.antoniaswinson.co.uk

Typeset by Waverley Typesetters, Galashiels
Printed and bound in the United Kingdom by Creative Print & Design, Wales

$£$£$£$£$£$£$£$£$£

CONTENTS

To my son Rory,
who turns pennies into pounds,
and life into a party.

$£$£$£$£$£$£$£$£$£

ACKNOWLEDGEMENTS

T HERE are so many people I should thank in the writing of this book, not least members of the public, who have given me so many ideas and suggestions at my workshops and talks, and two fellow writers Fred Harrison and Keith Cahill, who encouraged me when the going was tough. I have been extraordinarily lucky to have had imaginative editors, who let me write for the sheer fun of it and a supremely encouraging publisher, Ann Crawford, who left me in peace to write the book over a harsh Edinburgh winter. Thanks are also due too to Alison Fleming for all her big-picture ideas; and Ann Vinnicombe for her patience. Back on the home front, as I pounded away on my keyboard, the floor covered with books and papers, my children, Rory and Ella, coped wonderfully with gallons of home-made soup, because I had no time to visit the shops, and, finally, my biggest thanks are reserved for my husband Alan Reid, whose kindness, love and support deserve a long-service medal and whose rare creativity is beyond price.

1

$£$£$£$£$£$£$£$£

INTRODUCTION

THE wind is howling outside the window. The tea and biscuits are long finished and I am standing in front of fifty people, about to start a speech, nervously folding over the corners of my notes. Before me, I can see large leather handbags leaning against chairlegs and expectant faces. It is a cold, winter Monday afternoon in a small east-coast Scottish town and I am addressing a local church group. The jolly title which the Chairman had suggested would fill the hall is 'God and Money: is it possible to be a financial journalist and a Christian?' Originally, I thought this sounded good fun; it had to be better than spending an afternoon pounding a keyboard. But now, looking around, I am suddenly not so sure. Anything that mixes God and Money has to mean dicing with death, like Daniel in the lion's den.

I start off gently dishing up a happy youth in late 1980s' London spent interviewing celebrities. I lob famous names into the room like chocolate éclairs and they are gobbled up: bumping into Princess Di, Fergie, Marti Caine, John Major, Hooray Henrys knocking back 'Bolly' in the City. Robbie Coltrane and that red-head in Abba. Absolutely Fabulous! (It seems an age away.) I recount my first afternoon writing for the personal finance pages of the *Daily Express*; I had moved over from the women's pages, thinking it would be an interesting change. Two p.m., and I am standing in the ladies' loo in the old *Express* building on Fleet Street, dubbed the

1

'Black Lubyanka', having a panic attack; I have to write 800 words on alternative investments by 4.55 p.m. and I do not know anything about anything. The door opens and the late, great columnist Jean Rook sweeps in, immaculate as ever, to find me in full meltdown. She wastes no time mixing cold water on my face with this good advice: 'Never underestimate the advantage of total ignorance and the power of the simple question.'

I tell my audience that I have never forgotten this advice; it has saved my skin more than once. So I ask, 'Do you think anyone *can* be a financial journalist and a Christian?'

Fortified by strong tea and gingernuts, my audience burst out laughing. 'You'd have to be obsessed with money to do that for a living,' announces another. 'Aye, money is the root of all evil, hen!' comes a voice from the back of the room. Gales of laughter. 'Render unto Caesar that which is Caesar's and unto God that which is God's,' quotes another. She isn't laughing, but everyone else thinks I'm a scream. How can she possibly think she can be a financial journalist of all things, writing about money and markets, *and* say she's a Christian? Music-hall phrases spring to mind about being no better than I ought to be. (What does that actually mean?)

I stand there suddenly facing that vast disconnection between God and unrighteous Mammon. Mind the gap. I remember that nasal phrase repeated every time an Underground train arrives in London's Victoria Station. Mind the gap. Mind the gap. How could I possibly think I could bridge it?

Yet, gaps are my stock in trade. Daring myself to leap over them is an occupational necessity. Gaps are like a sum waiting to be added up, a 2 + 2. Gaps left unexplained, unminded; gaps are the stuff of fraud; gaps let people off the hook for, if you don't take account of something, it doesn't count. Gaps are also loopholes that always help someone to get ahead. Yet what could be a more extraordinary sum for any financial journalist? God + Money = Trouble. Now there's an angle.

Thinking on my feet now. I ask whether as investors, savers and debtors a belief in God can help us to understand money better? In a cut-throat market economy, can that still, small voice of calm and conscience prevent us from being schmoozed into one of the herd, whipped up into a froth of greed and fear? Can God help us think for ourselves amid the fraudulent hype sometimes handed out by the most plausible-sounding professionals?

In fact, I suggest, let us turn the question round. Can any of us make sense of money without having spiritual values at the heart of our decision-making? Why do we have such an ambivalence to God and Money? Loads of us in the rich West are up to our necks in mortgage debt and credit-card statements, paying out hundreds in monthly interest payments. Yet all this activity seems to be ring-fenced from God, as if it is none of his business. Is this why so often we don't ask ourselves who is profiting at our expense and what our debt habit is doing to us spiritually? We plough spare cash into tax-efficient equity vehicles, which invest in God knows what companies, which in turn affect communities, God knows how; we certainly don't. What do we care as long as we get a good return?

Jesus took a very dim view of exploitative financial services. His 'render unto Caesar' line, in answer to a trick question from those well-heeled enemies, was surely not designed to let Christians off the hook, but to teach us that we need a balanced portfolio in our lives, of the worldly and the spiritual.

This big gap that we have allowed to open up between God and money is a wonderful example of how we want God in our lives, but not too close. For money is more intimate than sex, sought with more passion than true love, and it defines our innermost selves. When I moved from the women's pages into personal finance and business journalism, I quickly learned that while people happily volunteer the most technicolour details of their sex lives, they are silent about their income and their real expenditure. Money is secret. Few of us would discuss our income with our children, let alone a journalist. It is too personal, it's all about us and how much money we have, or aspire to have, it dictates the threshold of our every relationship.

Heads nod in the long silence that follows. Oh, dear. Heavy stuff for a Monday afternoon: God, Money and now I have managed to mention S.E.X. as well. Hastily, I retreat into celebrity tales: the day my two-year-old son pressed the redial button on my phone and ended up having a long chat with Jackie Collins's PA in Beverly Hills; the day I went up for a gossip on the Upper East Side in the lair of American society writer Dominick Dunne . . .

'Thank you, Miss Swinson, for your most interesting talk. I'm sure we'd *all* like to show our appreciation. Ladies! Wouldn't we?'

I am walking home. It is not yet five o'clock but it is already dark. Fragments of words and noises blow in off the sea: thoughts of widows and mites, camels wedged in the eyes of needles, money-changers' tables crashing on to stone flags in the Temple. The biting wind cutting in off the Firth of Forth suddenly throws me against a wall; salt air whips my face. God and Money, what a subject. The bottom line is that I am certain that money, the stuff we think about dozens of times a day, is on the front line in our battle to find an honest relationship with God. And it can be a battle too, with blood on the carpet. Then the wind dashes out a £60 contact lens from my left eye. It has been a costly afternoon.

This book has been gestating ever since. No, that verb is far too ladylike as a description. Whizzing, fizzing, sizzling, bubbling, steaming away in the background as, lucky me, I have been paid to interview other people about their attitudes to money and write bolshy controversial columns about markets and sectors. What an extraordinary financial rollercoaster we have lived through, as one millennium tipped into another.

The proposal for this book, and the opening chapters, started off quite sweet and gentle, but somehow it gathered claws as the months went on. Covering two of the world's biggest subjects in just 80,000 words means omissions, for brevity concentrates on the art of the possible. If other expert books deal with third-world debt and other world faiths' financial attitudes, that is fine by me. I am a writer, I want people to buy lots of other writers' books. This cheeky scratchy animal of a book, however, is written by a financial journalist, and is based on my own work and experience, with case studies that have had the biggest effect on me and my readers.

Ask yourself: is this individual, company, church, school, relationship or friendship true and honest? Truly honest? Or are they fundamentally dishonest? If it is dishonest then, in spite of all benefits they might give you, dishonesty will always run through like words on a stick of rock. Somehow we must find the confidence to handle this dishonesty with which we inevitably interact in our everyday life, without losing our own sure footing and the faith to seek out honesty. That is why we need to employ our spiritual values in our financial life. That is why they count.

I am a Christian, and so it is within a Christian frame of reference that I set out to consider some of the big systems that underpin our financial lives, and ask the simple questions. Or perhaps I should rephrase this and say that I try hard to be one. Now, this is not to say that the Christian Church is immune from financial bad practice. Indeed, like all mature institutions, it needs constant vigilance and good faith to guard against complacency, greed, cronyism and corruption. As a believer, I have also had more than my fair share of doubts, dissension and despair, yet Christianity remains the faith, for better or worse, on which I base my life.

There is a 'cussedness' about Jesus' reaction to money, according to James Buchan, as if seeing money as a competitive authority.[1] There is something in this, I fear, for in Christians' ambivalence to God and Money – rendering unto Caesar and God separate dues – they have developed over centuries a most expensive disconnection, one which has been filled up by poverty, indebtedness and political impotence.

This dual-track world view has somehow driven us to consider the financial and the spiritual as separate systems: one dirty, the other clean; one for the working week and the other for Sundays. People of other faiths seem to enjoy a more worldly, connected, healthy relationship with money. So, here are some simple questions. If there is a breach between God and unrighteous Mammon in the Christian faith, whom has it suited? Whom has it enriched or made more powerful? What systems has this rift created, under which we now must live? Just what and how much have we given away?

In financial journalism, the old adage when digging information is always follow the money! I pass on this advice gratis. When looking at any person or organisation, not least our churches and any suspiciously holier-than-thou Christian, whether holding public office or in private life, always follow the money. Follow it to see how and why it is made and then spent, for it is only through tracking down where the money goes, that we learn the true picture. For money is the energy that flows where we most want it to, whatever we may say to cover our tracks. Balance sheets and government statistics can be bibles or just best-selling fiction in the truth they reveal or conceal. Of course they can sell us a line, but as the great investor genius Warren Buffett has observed, you never know who has been swimming naked till the tide goes out. Follow the money and in the end we always find out who is winning, who harmed and exploited. Nothing else so clearly exposes personal or corporate wiles, our aspirations and desires, our success or failure to live God's way.

This is the reason why we have to connect God and Money, why we must make our spiritual values count, because we can't afford not to. Somehow, we must leap over that false gap of disinformation between the two worlds, and make sense of how money fits into our spiritual lives. This does mean leaping over controversial minefields; I confess this book will take us into dangerous territory and I do question some accepted financial norms, which will have some few readers shaking with rage or disbelief. However, this book is also a personal journey born of hard work and personal experience. But frankly, what else can you expect? A book by a journalist titled *Root of All Evil?* has a to be a cheeky beast, by nature set to walk on the wild side.

Two observations to fortify us for this journey.

Number one: we shall never have enough money in our whole lives to satisfy us. Never. Human nature is never satisfied. There's always some undeserving swine up the aisle or at the other end of the office who is richer than us, with more bedrooms in his or her house and more shares, and it's not fair! Even multi-millionaires, after a few drinks, look over their shoulders and whinge about others' bigger fortunes, land banks and market share. I know, because I've met them.

Number two (always useful in a downturn this): whatever the anorexic state of our bank accounts, pensions and investments, however often the world and our bank manager write us off, God never disinvests. He is in the market for the long term. To him, we have a triple A rating. So come with me. Don't mind the gap. Jump . . . !

2

$£$£$£$£$£$£$£$£$£

THE CHILDHOOD OF MONEY

ALL the press pack are there at EMI's London offices. Flash! Questions are snatched from the air, besuited record-company executives guard their property like bull mastiffs with a quarterpounder. It is 2 October 2002. Robbie Williams is announcing that he has signed to stay with EMI, for a rumoured record sum of £80 million. City analysts are described as 'surprised' – Cityspeak translation: aghast – given EMI's 1,800 lay-offs and £20 million pay-off to Mariah Carey. But no matter; EMI has fought off rivals Sony and Virgin, and now Robbie, tattooed and smiling, is here to entertain us. Eyes and teeth! Flash! His manager claims that this is a watershed deal that will make a positive change to the workings of the music industry. Well, he would say that, wouldn't he? Robbie's last album *Swing When You're Winning* sold 5.4 million copies, despite not being available in the USA; just think what a future lies before him! Eighty million smackers ... Robbie punches the air. But when asked to confirm the figure ... Go on, give us a soundbite for the early evening news, Robbie. He is suddenly coy and refuses to confirm the figure. 'My mum said it would be really uncouth to talk about money, but I'm rich beyond my wildest dreams.' Rich!

Clever positioning. Robbie Williams as cheeky wee boy, rather than corporate fat cat, or greedy celebrity. How extra-ordinary are the rules that govern financial envy?

We allow Cinderellas and Aladdins to be rich, for they are the stuff of our childhood. We interact with these huge numbers as if we are still children even though, deep down, we know this is only a global business trying to make money out of us like any other. Like Robbie, however, we care what his mum thinks – not that we know her, nor want to, but because in his seeking her approbation, we see a mirror image of our own relationship. 'Uncouth.' Now there's an interesting adjective for someone dripping with street cred. Robbie leaps in the air. The press pack loved him for it. For he lives our dreams, doesn't he? How do you feel Robbie? Magic. Rich beyond his wildest dreams? The stuff of fairytales. Even if it does not take long for tabloid headlines to surface about the singer losing £2 million in a casino with an expensive £50,000 a pop dice-throwing habit.

EMI's shareholders naturally are far from enchanted. The stock ends the day 1 per cent down, after City analysts went on the record to describe the recording deal as 'bizarre'.

Here we have the two worlds of money interior and exterior coming together in a good TV soundbite. 'My mum says' juxtaposes with '80 million quid'! Wealth beyond anyone's wildest dreams is set against men in grey suits looking jumpy at the edge of the screen waiting for the market's dour reaction.

Far away from our bank manager, our insurance broker, our independent financial adviser, our employer, staff, colleagues and partners and children – let us ask ourselves what we really feel about money deep, deep down. Feel. Not think.

Psychotherapist and writer Dorothy Rowe wisely observes that understanding money means understanding ourselves.[1] Yet I would take this further and say that it is only when we understand ourselves and our attitudes to money that we can understand our relationship with God. What a sum. Yet what a risk we run if we don't try. For it is the disconnection between sense and emotion, between our honesty and with God and ourselves, which can be so easily exploited by others – to our cost.

So let us step back into our childhood, when we were at our most powerless and dependent on the good will of others and most easily influenced. Let us see what messages we imbibed, and which we then carried, for good or ill, into our adult life, only to give, in turn, to our own children. Warning: this is not an easy calculation.

I suspect God and Money enter our lives when we are young children at roughly the same time, as we are beginning to make sense of the world around us and establish the boundaries of our control over it. Fewer and fewer children are taken to church today, and yet God, along with other supernatural beings, such as the tooth fairy and Santa Claus, starts figuring in a child's world view. At the same time, along comes the emotional maelstrom which surrounds pocket money, with all those mixed messages about thrift and whether or not we deserve it.

As for grown-ups' money, it is between the ages of four and six that it seems we start growing large-flapping ears. Why not? Money is fascinating and seems to be talked about everywhere around us; it is so often the stuff of most grown-up conversation, of every children's story.

In her book, *The Secret Life of Money*, Valerie Wilson looks at everyday money language, and notes the emotionally loaded nature of the words we use, ranging from virtue and purity, right through the spectrum to dirt and promiscuity, which we pick up so quickly as children.[2] Very early on we find ourselves saying the odd sentence our parents tell us, that money 'doesn't grow on trees', as if we ever thought it did! Unlike goodies and baddies in books and cartoons, money is strange because it seems to be both good and bad. So we can splash our pennies from Heaven while listening to grown-ups knocking the 'filthy' rich for their 'easy' money, taking 'everyone to the cleaners'. It is all very confusing.

Look at the number of expressions that surround money and motherhood, babies, milk and food that reflect childhood experience. So we feather our nests with our nest egg, hopefully after milking our cash cows, while all the time putting our money where our mouth is . . .

Wilson goes on to look at the cold, hard, emotion-free nature of official language. Its balance and equity, its profit and loss, assets and liabilities. What strikes anyone who reads personal finance ads is how copywriters so cleverly play on our emotions – using the personal, everyday language we learned as children to maximum effect, evincing a childlike response, in order to flog more products in the impersonal, official money world. We need to be constantly on our guard for the gap between these two worlds, and the gatekeepers who profit from it: such as the independent financial advisers (IFAs), the banks and the product providers.

By the age of eight, we are already learning to evaluate just what is value for money. And this calculation is directly bound up to our feelings of self-worth, how loved we feel, how cherished and nurtured, or rejected and fearful. This subjective calculation remains as hard to shift in adult life as our attitudes to food.

I have interviewed dozens of people over the years about money: billionaires and beggars; people living on tick, others with thousands in the bank who dress from Oxfam. Without fail, their early experiences with money are vivid and revealing, establishing financial patterns for good or ill, providing a yardstick for value, against which their later success or failure is measured. When these people talk of their childhood, their language becomes descriptive, they recall the sayings about money their parents told them. Often these parental experiences with money are branded on their soul.

The historical novelist, the late Nigel Tranter, recalled how his father, a Church of Scotland minister, was made to honour a £65,000 debt he had guaranteed, forcing him to leave the Church. The year was 1906; the sum was a fortune, representing about £1.5 million in today's money. The trauma affected Nigel Tranter throughout his life with a desperate horror of debt; mortgages for him were a fearsome proposition. Award-winning writer A. L. Kennedy found the mathematics of debt horrific, having once had a strict maths teacher at primary school who made the class complete exercises in compound interest for three weeks. She was so horrified at the unfairness of it that she was determined to save and take on as little debt as possible.

Others associated early money memories with physical hardship. Bank Chairman Fred Goodwin recalled seeing a Dynatron stereo in a shop window for £100. He worked all summer on a building site to get it, while football coach Craig Brown remembered the biting cold when gathering firewood in the forest, which he sold at a penny a bundle. Former Episcopal Primus Bishop Richard Holloway spent all his pocket money on comics. Once he was given a half-crown coin, but it accidentally rolled down a drain and he was inconsolable. The late Lord Younger recalled his mother writing down every penny spent on housekeeping, useful programming for the future Chairman of the Royal Bank of Scotland. Breakfast TV's hostess Lorraine Kelly, daughter of a TV repair man, talked affectionately of having plenty of money – while growing up in the Gorbals.[3]

Attitudes to money are generational. Anyone over fifty-five will recall the crushing need to remain respectable, in spite of food rationing and the horror of falling through the social fabric because of debt. The Second World War also created attitudes to pooling financial resources. Others brought up with plenty exhibited a certain financial élan. I recall TV cook Clarissa Dickson Wright in our interview giving me the memorable advice that bankruptcy was rather like losing your virginity. It is never so frightening the second time![4]

Give me a child till age of eight and he is mine for life, runs the wise old Jesuit line. For most of us, by the age of eight, spending patterns are established, composed of hidden messages culled from family and peers, and reflecting our position in the family. Let us step outside ourselves and look at these patterns, for it is extraordinary how effective they are at conditioning our behaviour.

Take a very common issue: financial competition between the generations. Those parents who were brought up before or during the Second World War continue to exert a power balance that does not shift as they get older, because of the financial muscle conferred by the high asset prices of their houses. This has an extraordinary effect of grown-up professional children remaining fixed in pocket-money mode with their parents. Ask yourself who benefits from this disconnection which can run on for decades? As always, it is the people with the assets.

Then there are the patterns of money we learn from this power play. How many of us had fathers who encouraged financial ignorance in their wives? Whom did this disconnection between money and information suit? Yes, the husband, for his power in the marriage is secure. It can also happen the other way round, with the wife holding the purse strings. Money is power. Think of William Thackeray's observation that in every relationship there are those who love and those who consent to be loved. Into that axis falls money.

Looking back in my press cuttings, over years of interviews, there are three lines that seem to predominate in that mixed bag of homily and hypocrisy children receive for free. 'Do as I say, not as I do' and 'What's yours is mine, what's mine is mine,' and 'Don't tell your father/mother/ granny.' Grown-ups promise rewards, lecture us on thrift, and then splurge out on extraordinary things. They tell us not to lie, and yet we notice how smoothly they fib. 'It only cost X,' they say, straightfaced. (We note this for future reference.)

Mothers, even in these liberated times, will stuff shopping bags under the stairs so their partners can't see them. Children take note. Frustratingly, parents will happily tell stories about their childhood, but never divulge how much they earn, which is what we really want to know. How much is a lot? Or a little. Are we richer or poorer than so and so's dad? How come he has a bigger car than we?

No wonder our childhood experience of money is confusing, hacking through such a jungle of adult hypocrisy. Yet we must do it, for, otherwise, how else can we establish what is value for money? It is these childhood messages that mean we splurge on food, but consider a CD or theatre ticket as wasteful. Why we forego small comforts for ourselves, while spending on others; or the other way round.

What a cocktail of guilt, instant or delayed gratification, reward and punishment. When is money real or pretend? How can grown-ups spend money they don't have? When is debt not a debt? When it is turned, as if by magic, into credit, like a pumpkin into a fairy coach. Children quickly adapt to this smoke-and-mirrors fiscal universe and learn to negotiate expectations and outcomes with a subtlety worthy of an Alan Greenspan, Chairman of the Board of Governors of the Federal Reserve System.[5] We can spot irrational exuberance miles off and, as we hone our skills in emotional blackmail, make our pitch at just the right moment.

My own particular expertise in wangling expensive goodies out of my doting father was learned by the time I started school. I knew always to wait until my father had knocked back his second Dubonnet, after a hard day's work. Never the first, always the second. I would watch his shoulders gradually coming down from his ears, he would lean back, close his eyes, smile . . . then I would pounce! My elder sister, a more forthright character, never seemed to understand the timing and finesse needed when asking for money. So I became the first five-year-old in our town to own a bunny furcoat and she was refused a new pony. Another lesson learned early: when it comes to money, life is absolutely unfair!

An exercise. Let's shut our eyes and say, 'Money'.

I have run workshops on spirituality and money and it is fascinating that, when I ask people to do this, the answers are always similar, whatever the age or background of the audience. There are vivid descriptions of treasure chests of gold doubloons, or piles of crisp new banknotes in a briefcase, or those showers of fivers often used in TV ads for tabloid newspaper competitions. When I do this exercise, I see myself once again as a Brownie Guide, carefully counting all my silver shillings from 'Bob a Job' week into a large Elastoplast tin.

Why pre-decimal coinage, when I have spent years writing about the markets? And how come, now we're all so grown up with all our financial services, do we rarely picture money as a credit card? Or as a share certificate or mortgage statement, or even as a cheque? Money is transferred in trillions each day, swirling through cyberspace at the click of a mouse, yet childlike, we continue to picture money in our minds' eye as real, connected to us still, something we can hold in our hands. The joy of cash! The crumpling, satisfying feel of the real folding stuff of childhood.

Children and money. Always a fruitful line of enquiry for personal finance journalists like me, who can write usefully about savings products, mortgages and National Savings. But these products are merely expressions of the exterior world of money, which has nothing to do with our emotional inner world.

However, it is in writing fiction that one can enter the mind of a character and see just what the child inside really feels about money. And how it can drive the story forward.

In a scene in a novel I wrote, Katya Holland, a twenty-four-year-old conceptual artist, is at the opening night of an exhibition at a gallery in London's East End.[6] The show, titled 'The Real Meaning of Money', is sponsored by a (fictional) City merchant bank. This is an edgy, emotionally disconnected character, whose feuding parents both share the characteristic of pouring any spare cash down other people's throats, as well as their own. Katya is not comfortable company for merchant bankers, but she is as desperate for money as they are; the idea for her art installation came from a short item I read a few years ago, in the London *Evening Standard*.

[Katya's] own commission was causing ructions. She'd adapted an old slide projector. Visitors could touch a button and bank statements and loan arrangements and other financial details would appear onto a large screen. People were laughing for here were cashcard payments to the off-licence, to the Caprice restaurant . . . a four figure direct hit for the mortgage, and so on and on. A fascinating glimpse at others' financial stew. She had found the actual statements outside the back entrance of the Bank's Piccadilly branch. There had been poorly tied bin bags waiting for the dustmen. The bags were too full and had slit, the wind threatening to decant them into the street. Hundreds of customer records were potentially on view, details of overdrafts and loan arrangements. Had banks never heard of shredders? She had taken them home and had inked out the bank's logo and the names, though through the bank's carelessness, she now had details of hundreds of customers' financial details. Some very well known customers indeed. How careless of an M.P. to actually put through cashcard payments for a massage parlour. She could have cleared her overdraft selling it to the Sunday tabloids.

Every sixth button press showed up a card which explained how the statements had been found. Then the smiles would suddenly fade. The execs would never know whether they had come from their bank or not, though by the worried looks she knew they probably did. A little joke on our sponsors . . . Customers went into the marble floored front of the bank, bursting with solidity, integrity and trust and then their personal details and records, for want of the cost of a shredder, were excreted into cheap plastic bin bags for Westminster Council to clear up. A perfect metaphor. Whereas money itself was pure energy flowing through buildings and lives for good or ill . . .

How this cold and self-contained girl finds peace and success makes for an interesting journey. My other characters have surprised me with their secret bank accounts and covert spending habits. As fictional characters come alive, they become – to use Italian playwright Luigi Pirandello's observation, 'meno reali ma più vivi' – less real but more alive. Naturally they develop interior financial lives, just as we do in real life. A fascinating opportunity for novelists, dabbling in their characters' innermost thoughts. Whereas in real life, even with our spouses and closest relations, the interior money life remains an off-limits world, usually only ever exposed after death. If then.

Our childhood money memories are usually among our most vivid, fixed in our culture, time and place. Here are two money memories from the United States. The first is from a retired army administrator now living in northern California; the second is from the leading American environmental writer Erich Hoyt.

CHILDHOOD MEMORIES FROM THE USA

1) I was born in 1935 in Pacific Beach, Washington. Three blocks farther west from our house and you entered the Pacific Ocean, which was very rough and very cold. I never understood why it was named the Pacific, which I was told meant calm. The population was 500 if you counted the dogs and the cats, and my grandparents had lived in this town since my mother was two years old in 1919. We were surrounded by water and trees, and livings were made by fishing and lumber. There was no bank in our town and one of my primary teachers gave many of us our first concept of how banks operated by banking money for us.

My pa worked in the shingle mill, which went out on strike every so often, and we charged our groceries all of the time at the store in the little town where I lived. Some people went to the nearest city to buy cheaper groceries but I was told the small store carried our bill if there was a strike and we would buy there all the time because of that. That is not exactly learning about money, but it is learning about being fair in your dealings with businesses and people. And I wonder now, in retrospect, if it was ma that insisted on that.

Ma and pa never spoke about money in front of me – not $100 or 25 cents. They never told me anything about budgeting, because they did not do it. Pa told me that it would not matter how much money he earned, Ma would spend all of it. Unfortunately, he was right.

When I was pregnant, I had no insurance and I paid money to both the doctor and the hospital every pay-day while I was pregnant and had most of the charges paid when the baby was born. When I really learned something about money, I asked my parents to loan me some money (I do not remember how much or what it was for) and they did not have it. I knew that their parents had money in the bank and I knew they should have had money in the bank and I became a vigorous saver.

2) I was brought up North Virginia and would spend my allowance on Reese's Peanut Buttercups, Baby Ruth's Candy Bars and coins for my collection. In the 1950s, you could get 1890 silver dollars. They were precious. One day, my brother raided my collection and bought ice cream for the whole neighbourhood with one of my special dollars. But just at its face value. It was worth $62.50. I can still see the ice cream van driving down the street and feel the gall and rage I had for my brother. The driver didn't come back. He knew he had struck lucky. The neighbours still talk about his generosity. I guess it taught me not to cling on to possessions as sacred.

Such memories are the stuff of stories, and as with all good stories, we learn from them.

Let us write down the key experiences from the first two decades of our lives and then consider the patterns or connections that pertain to our recent financial dealings. The result can be surprising, for we are not half as cool and objective as we think. And there lies the danger. For unless we understand ourselves and why we use and sometimes abuse money as we do, we are prey to the emotive language of people who earn their living flogging us financial services, all of whom are trained to see soft spots in our psyche. Now there are many good independent financial advisers around, but watch out, they can play us like violins, such is our childlike vulnerability about our personal money, however much of it we manage at work; just read their trade papers. Words like 'security', 'prudent' and 'permanence' work a treat if you had a childhood that was marked by a lack of love. For others, words like 'quality' or 'cutting edge' or 'high return' can work for those who experienced greater emotional and material plenty, who feel they can afford to lose more. Then there is, as I have said, all that fluffy talk of nest eggs, which can make us feel loved and all warm inside.

It doesn't hurt to tell your own money memories as a story. So now, speeding back in time, I return to my own childhood, yes, another country where they spend differently . . .

I was brought up with my brother and sister a couple of minutes' walk from St Albans Cathedral in Hertfordshire in the south-east of England. My father, Arthur Swinson, was a successful full-time writer and military historian. He always had two or three projects on the go at any one time and averaged 5,000 words a day.

My mother ran a small charity, a children's arts centre, where we children painted, sang, acted and learned poetry. Looking back, we had sky-high living standards. In a good year, my father would earn as much as £10,000, a fortune in the days when a headmaster earned £1,500. Both parents enjoyed spending on others, but they were also careful, checking statements and filing away bills in date order. My father was always worried about money, such a lot was riding on his creativity; but I remember the shock he had one day, when he found out that some friends in our church were living on a constant overdraft. For him, living on debt as a matter of habit, without making every effort to pay it off quickly, was a sin.

Fund-raising for the arts centre was a big family activity. One day, when I was six, I sneaked out of the house and started knocking on doors, rattling a cocoa tin to collect money for the arts centre. I did this three times one Saturday, and my parents became so worried by Sunday morning, they were demanding to know where I had been. By that time, I had been all over the neighbourhood and now had £3 16s 3d stored up in a cardboard box. A lot of money, perhaps as much as £50 today in spending power. In those days, the terrors of paedophiles were not such a concern. My mother was touched and thrilled by my initiative; my father was horrified that I had been out collecting door to door without a licence. An interesting difference of perspective. I was made to promise never to do such a thing again. I shall always remember those heavy threepenny bits and the thrilling power of suddenly discovering I had the ability to persuade grown-ups to part with their money for a good cause.

Though my father had to pay the extraordinary high top tax rate, life was good in the 1960s. We had foreign holidays, ponies and ballet lessons. The milk that Ernie the milkman delivered (his real name!) had a navy-blue top with the gold bar, 100 per cent full-cream Jersey milk. But, as a general rule, money was not discussed; this was vulgar. One did not read bills at the end of restaurant meals either, and it was also vulgar for children to have their own post-office accounts. We never asked why, we just accepted it as gospel.

Not that our lifestyle was due to unearned income. In my father's family, money had been tight with five children, his own father having died as a child. My father, like so many writers, wrote for dear life: 300 radio plays for the BBC in under a dozen years, and more than thirty books and several hit TV series including *Dr Finlay's Casebook.* He died, exhausted of a heart attack, on holiday in Spain, aged just fifty-four.

Only then, when I was thirteen, did I begin to understand money. To lose a parent is the end of a world. Nothing is ever the same again. And so the navy-blue milk with the gold stripe became gold top, then silver. The man from the tax office came to value my father's clothes for death duties, and my mother, a pretty blonde in her mid-thirties, was informed that it was legal for snoopers from the benefits office to put a ladder up against the house wall to climb up, to see if there were men's pyjamas on the pillow: evidence of a man in the house meant her Widow's Benefit would be stopped. She had not even known that the house was not in their joint names.

I remember taking old pewter tankards round the local antique shops to sell for cash, before my father's will was settled. Then so-called friends of the family, many from our church, started offering cash advances, for the family assets, for our mastiff dog, our Hillman Hunter car, our beautiful Georgian home. There were other advances, too, which also had to be fended off; par for the course, I learned later as a journalist, when a household loses the male provider and protector. What also seemed to me extraordinary was how quickly we were dropped socially by people who had enjoyed so much of my parents' attention and hospitality. Most people have to go through redundancy or divorce as adults before they realise quite what a proportion of their friendships are based merely on how much lifestyle spending, or reflected glory they can provide.

It made for a fast growing up, which put a value on money as insulation and protection, but gave importance, too, to that more priceless asset, time – spent with people you love, because life is short. A challenging balance sheet to achieve in this workaholic world, and these early experiences conditioned many of my professional and financial decisions. But the biggest asset of any writer is experience, whether good or bad, drenched in money or not; none is ever wasted.

Think about the books we loved as children and the money messages they contained. Human nature never changes and money *is* the stuff of fairytales taught to us from the cradle, which try a grown-up life on for size, with all its financial twists and turns. The tale of Cinderella is as much a star piece of financial fiction, as a romance. Cinders may end up with her prince, but the fact she gets out of rags and into a palace matters as much. In my brief but enjoyable early career as an actress, I played Cinderella twice nightly for three months at the famous Glasgow Pavilion for £175 a week during a freezing west-coast winter. The great music-hall star Marie Lloyd had played the Pavilion for years and went down in Glasgow showbusiness history. She was known for coming out of the stage door on pay day and scattering gold coins to the waiting adoring crowds.

So, as I stepped shivering from my rags into my gorgeous ball gown and back into rags for the second show, I would find myself thinking more about Cinders' financial elevation than her love life. What happened to her once she had the keys to the palace? One night Cinders nearly did not get her Prince; my chilblains were so bad, Dandini could barely jam the crystal slipper on, very nearly leading to the unexpected financial elevation of the smaller of two Ugly Sisters! The actor playing Cinders' father was the late Bill Simpson of *Doctor Finlay's Casebook* fame. For his entrance, he had to go onstage and announce, 'I'm Baron Hard-Up.' Opening night, he played the line and quick as a shot came inimitable Glaswegian repartee from the back of the stalls, 'You must be, pal!'

Beauty and the Beast is another piece of financial fiction; Beauty may have had to take on the Beast, but as her merchant father had lost his money, pragmatism was called for and, by the end of the story, she is mistress of some prize gothic real estate. Even Snow White, who finds her prince in a rather instant fashion at the end of the story, nevertheless learns to earn her own living as housekeeper to seven dwarfs.

The tales of Snow White and Cinderella both teach children of the financial difficulties of second marriages, when resources must be split between two families. What could be more relevant today? In a darker vein, Hansel and Gretel perform an inter-generational asset smash-and-grab raid, by pushing the old witch into the oven and making off with her jewels, and then returning to the starving woodcutter.

All the best children's books are rolling in money. So today's children enjoy the fact that Harry Potter has his piles of galleons in Gringott's Bank to sustain him, while Jacqueline Wilson's streetwise heroine Tracey Beaker may live in a children's home, but she has a financial nous that could buy and sell the Artful Dodger.

When I was young, I learned all about budgeting and poverty from Eve Garnett's *Family at Number One, One End Street*, with the valiant struggles of Mr Ruggles the dustman to provide for his seven children in 1930s' Depression. My grandmother gave me her own ancient copy of the Victorian classic *How Paul's Penny Became A Pound*, the engravings of a lacy-collared little boy carefully saving his pennies which inspired me to save, while Enid Blyton's Noddy taught me economics for the self-employed. *Harriet & The Cherry Pie* was the most magical Puffin classic for my generation, which explained exactly why a business had to make profits, and *The Railway Children* in Technicolor showed us that losing all your money and domestic help, when your father went to prison, could be fun. Yet, in practical terms, many of my generation left school without the vaguest notion of how to run a current account. Nowadays, children are taught about third-world debt at primary school, with money management packs shipped in from the high-street banks yet, as students, they could accrue debts the size of what perhaps some people paid for their first house. So the generation gap yawns open ever wider. However the question – what is value for money? – remains as intimate and as conditional as ever.

So the bottom line is, what do we really feel inside about money? Can we ever have enough presents or teddy bears or sweets – for which read houses, cars and designer clothes – because only these may fill the hole where love should have been? Do we fear they will be taken away? Do we feel only as good as the goods we own? Do we 'scqwweam' like Just William's nemesis, Violet Elizabeth Bott, if we cannot have the goodies that we want? Or do we feel money always comes along when we need it? Back in touch with those feelings and memories, yet with an adult understanding, perhaps we can now start to regain our trust in God and ask him where we go next?

For money should be a joy we use, not our master cracking the whip over us. Keith Tondeur of Credit Action, in his excellent book *Your Money and Your Life*, suggests that we should devise and then sign a form that hands over our assets and money to God and that makes us merely stewards of his wealth.[7] He also suggests talking about this money in terms of 'Your' and 'His' rather than 'my' and 'mine'. This is great advice, for this process delivers an extraordinary transformation; every penny we spend now becomes a spiritual decision.

This is not easy to do but, if we try it, we can feel the pressure coming off our shoulders. Handing our money over is hugely liberating. We are no longer insecure misers with our stash, but stewards with responsibility and free will, who are in control. As stewards, we are less likely to lose a bundle on the 3.15 race at Doncaster through self-hatred, or indulge in comfort-seeking. In this role we might also manage to give away a bit more money as well – sometimes so much harder to do than wasting it.

Stewardship is the process of reconnecting God and Money, with Love as glue. This is not wishful thinking, but hard-headed, money-saving advice. Is it really so mad? In such a world as this, why shouldn't spiritual values start counting – for our benefit?

For in our sophisticated grown-up world, our own money is rarely held in our own hands. Invisible, well-paid professionals manage it for us – and, by the way, still get their bonuses, even if they lose our money for us in incompetent investments – while the rest slips in and out of our bank account, in automatic pay-ins, direct debits and standing orders, to fund our bills and lifestyle.

Reconnecting money with God means taking back control, no longer living as children, impotent and on the receiving end of others, usually the ones with the vested interests or assets who profit at our expense. This self-promotion to

Steward immediately gives us permission to ask grown-up, tough questions about where our money goes and what it is used for. We may also connect with our own history, to those thrifty financial habits that saw our ancestors through good times and bad.

'For surely I know the plans I have for you, says the Lord, plans for your welfare and not for harm, to give you a future with hope.' What a quote from Jeremiah 29:11. And people write off his book as depressing! All we need is the confidence to assign our assets over to him. Once that contract is signed, money suddenly becomes real, as it used to be, in its proper place, to use for good. The sort of tangible money we once touched, fumbled and stacked as children, before it started bullying us and beating us over the head in sums that we could never add up, however hard we tried.

Why shouldn't our spiritual values give us a financial edge? Robbie Williams might one day find this idea, post-Gamblers Anonymous, as cool as 80 million quid in the bank. Now, there's a thought to make us feel rich!

3

$£$£$£$£$£$£$£$£$£

DEBT: THE SPIRITUAL DANGER OF A FOUR-LETTER WORD

5 FEBRUARY 2003. After a day toiling over a hot computer writing this book, it is fun to get out of the house, even on an icy winter night like this. I am the guest speaker of the Colinton Literary Society, one of the most successful and popular on Scotland's book scene. The event is being held in a well-heeled south Edinburgh suburb, in the same church hall as my daughter's Scottish Country Dancing class. I am relieved I shall not be doing an eightsome reel, for clearly I must be on my mettle; my audience is elderly, highly educated and extremely well read.

My topic is 'Money in Fact and Fiction': concentrating on my original research, which has revealed the financial secret life of writer Anthony Trollope.

I begin by explaining that it is patterns of financial behaviour that I find so fascinating, both as a journalist and as a writer of three novels, all of which have money as the central theme.[1] How often do we read stories in *The Financial Times* about breathtaking greed and fear that could so easily be the stuff of a good plot? As we read daily news reports of our contemporaries' fraud, greed, debt and extravagance, why should we be surprised that the best novels have characters and plots driven by finance? How grippingly debt, greed and fear can drive the plot and the characters' development! Little wonder, therefore, that the money-mad Victorians, whose greed for growth and consumption so clearly mirrors our own, should have produced writers of such enduring popularity as Thackeray, Dickens and Anthony Trollope – but more of the creator of the nefarious character Melmotte later.

Jane Austen, writing just as the Napoleonic Wars gave way to rampant post-war expansion, also threads debt and the fear of poverty throughout her stories. For if *Pride and Prejudice* is driven by the need to marry any unsuspecting man in possession of five thousand pounds a year, then the fear of what will happen to the Bennet property on Mr Bennet's death runs just as strongly in the family's dysfunction. In *Persuasion*, debt drives the Eliot family out of the family seat to Bath, against a backdrop of the new post-Waterloo economic order, while in *Sense and Sensibility*, a rich man's second family is hived off to a cottage, unable to afford sugar.

Later, Charles Dickens, a journalist who set out to change society's attitudes through fiction, also knew first hand the dangers of financial mismanagement; family circumstances reduced this young middle-class boy to toil in a blacking factory. *Little Dorrit, Nicholas Nickleby, David Copperfield* and *Oliver Twist* are all child heroes who fall headlong into poverty when their parents' sums don't add up.

Great Expectations is a fine Cinderella tale of snobbery and deceit, while *A Christmas Carol* shows the hellish effects of miserliness. Extraordinarily contemporary too, is *The Old Curiosity Shop*. The crowds on the New York harbourside grieved for Nell when they learned of her death. How much of this was a catharsis of pity and fear that the consequences of losing property could happen to them?[2]

I stop to take questions. A lady in her seventies asks what I think about the present levels of debt being carried by younger people today: so different from the experience of her own generation, and so very worrying. There is a murmur of recognition from the audience, who all look concerned.

I tell her that I believe the present levels of personal debt are horrific and historically unprecedented. We now owe £850 billion in mortgages and loans, approaching the thousand billion – £1 trillion – value of the entire UK economy. I also share my belief that debt robs people of creativity, peace of mind, and quality of family life; that the only way to live happily is to cut debt out of the balance sheet as much as possible, even if it means less lifestyle spending. I decide to leave unspoken the thought that, from personal experience, the great advantage of downsizing is that it does flush out the once 'close friends' who only like us for what we own or buy!

Even though this is a question I am often asked, on this evening I find myself feeling surprised. And it takes me a moment to understand why. What is different is the very new level of concern being shown by people of this generation. Because for years, as the market in shares and property assets boomed, the attitudes of older people to their children's debt levels have always seemed to me detached, bordering sometimes on the smug.

So, if we are talking about changing patterns of behaviour, what has brought about this change? It could only be the stock-market. At the time of writing, shares on the FTSE have plummeted more than 50 per cent from the dizzy heights of New Year's Eve 2000, in the steepest fall since the Second World War. As a result, these older people have apparently suddenly woken up, realising that their wealth in shares may never be recovered. Also, as their children's debt rises, a black hole on the family's collective balance sheet has unexpectedly opened up, which could swallow up more of the wealth that they have so assiduously built up since the 1960s through inheritance and a hard-working life.

The following day, events appear to confirm the imbalance of this generational difference. The national press carries a study by the London Business School which shows that there is only a 50–50 chance of shares on the FTSE 100 Index regaining 6900 by 2018, and that it will probably take far longer.[3] Another survey announces that there are more stock-market millionaires in select postal codes of south Edinburgh, where I live, than anywhere in the UK, apart from the smartest London districts.

On the same day, the Bank of England's Monetary Policy Committee reduces interest rates by a quarter of 1 per cent to 3.75 per cent, down to levels last seen in 1955, a time when many of my audience would have been setting up home and starting their families. Back then, Winston Churchill was prime minister and a new home cost £2,000, and a family car £800, but an office worker earned just £14 per week. The rate cut sparks widespread fears in the financial press that the authorities are playing with fire and that consumer debt, and the remortgaging business that sustains it, will boom even higher, leading inevitably, to a re-run of the 1990s' housing crash and widespread negative equity. It sends the FTSE index falling another 2 per cent towards its recent seven-year low.

Our forebears learnt the hard way that debt can be systemic, even inter-generational: something we overlook, because we are either too complacent or too busy shopping. It seems that the more we earn, and the higher our standard of living, so the further God may be removed from us. I include the following case study to show that if our spiritual values do not count in our financial dealings, then there is never a respite to financial pressure, and to our lifelong feelings of discontent. We become slaves to money, and it dictates the quality of all our relationships. The great Victorian writer Anthony Trollope went from having the bailiffs at the door and money-lenders hovering over his office chair to earning the equivalent of £5 million in today's money, yet, still, it was never enough. His obsession with money is crucial to understanding his work. Debt skewed his judgement and invented a false persona, which is still largely accepted today.

Case Study I: The Hidden Financial Life of Anthony Trollope (Or 'How Making a Fortune Is Never Enough Money Whatever Age We Live In')

However many economic cycles we live through, at whatever point we stop to take stock, it is always worth remembering that, when it comes to money, human nature never changes; whether it is on the level of personal money management or big-business wheeler-dealing, its complexities make fine material for any writer.

Arguably, the master of financial fiction is Anthony Trollope, whose forty-seven novels cover every sort of debt, sleaze and property struggle. It was while carrying out research for my third novel that I discovered that Anthony Trollope was not the stentorian, bearded Victorian we imagine, but was, in reality, Tony Trollope, a ducker and diver who kept his secret Scottish life – how he began a friendship with one of the most brilliant businessmen of his generation, George Burns – very quiet indeed.

This discovery happened in 1998, at the Mitchell Library in Glasgow, when my husband Alan Reid and I stumbled across incontrovertible evidence that showed that Anthony Trollope had planned and written the first part of *Barchester Towers* (his first bestseller), while holed up at the holiday home of George Burns, a leading government supplier to the Irish Postal Service. Burns needed insider information at a key time of post-office expansion. Trollope, at the time, was a newly promoted civil servant in the Irish Postal Service. In the Inverclyde Collection, there is an article from an 1889 edition of *The World* annotated by George Burns's granddaughter Caroline, which is an interview with George Burns's son John, the first Lord Inverclyde. Quote: 'Anthony Trollope thought out and wrote a great portion of *Barchester Towers* at Castle Wemyss.' A throw-away line, but at the time it struck me as odd. George Burns had been a well-known evangelical Christian who did not approve of novels. Yet Caroline's pithy observations, written in copperplate correctness, were an incredible find, giving one of those magic moments which, so much more precious than money, comes perhaps only once in a lifetime. It was extraordinary to realise that I was holding material that had been missed by four eminent biographers in the past twenty years, as well as every Trollopian scholar: this was material that would change our knowledge of how the novel that made Trollope a star came to be written.

No manuscript has survived of the first seven chapters of *Barchester Towers*. In a supremely diaried life, their creation has always been a mystery. Trollope vaguely described writing them in railway carriages with a board on his knee. Yet here, long after his death, a rich businessman, while trying to find something interesting to say to a journalist, was suggesting that Trollope had written and thought out the book at the Burns family holiday home. Why did no one know?

The point about gaps, as any fraud squad officer will tell you, is that they are usually deliberate, the dogs that do not bark. Over months buried in dusty documents, I gradually realised that the reason no one knew that this most English of novels had been written in Scotland was precisely because neither Tony Trollope nor George Burns wanted anyone to know the genesis of their thirty-year friendship. For at its heart was money.

When it comes to business corruption, the bigger the financial stake, the bigger the secrecy. This strange, long friendship was based not so much on cash for questions as super generous, secretive hospitality in return for insider information valuable enough to drive aggressive and deep-pocketed rivals out of business and deliver enormous financial benefit to the instigator. No wonder Trollope does not mention the Burns family in his autobiography and Burns carefully positions Trollope as his son's friend in his hagiographic biography by Edwin Hodder.

Let us look at the patterns of money. As I discussed in the previous chapter, childhood experiences lay down enduring lifelong patterns. Trollope, the son of an unsuccessful barrister, had an early life characterised by privation and poverty, the family finances permanently on the verge of bankruptcy. His account of the miseries he endured at Harrow, in his too-small uniform, are poignant and, when he was nineteen, the family had to flee from creditors to Bruges. The horrors of debt, and keeping up appearances without money, marked him. 'No other novelist has made the various worries connected with the want of money so prominent a feature in most of his stories.' A pertinent observation from *The Saturday Review* in 1865.

Through string-pulling by his mother, the writer Fanny Trollope, an original British superwoman, Trollope entered the postal service in London with a safe job for life on £90 per annum. Yet, like his father before him, lifestyle spending led to the money-lenders hovering over his office chair, not impressing his superiors. A £12 debt ballooned, with interest, to

£200; so similar to stories we hear today of 'alternative credit providers', who hover on doorsteps, extracting APRs of 1000 per cent. When a £3 Irish note, which had been placed in his safekeeping, disappeared without explanation, Trollope leapt before he was pushed: in 1841 he took a job in the Irish postal service.[4]

Follow the money. It always explains how people 'tick'. In Ireland, Tony Trollope turned over a new leaf. He worked hard and acquired a fiercesomely efficient reputation. In travelling around Ireland, he made good money on his expenses, and acquired a wife, whose own background of insecure finances more than matched his own. But, by 1854, Trollope was desperate. His civil service career had stalled, awaiting promotion to the post of Surveyor of the Northern District of Ireland. He was now approaching forty with a high-maintenance wife, and a taste for good living and hunting. His first novel, *The Warden*, had been unsuccessful and publishers were lukewarm about a second.

Enter, stage left, Glaswegian businessman George Burns, Chairman of the Cunard Steamship Company, who had, for years, made money by running mailboats to Ireland from Greenock, controlling flow of government and commercial information. Back in 1839, when a Boston merchant Samuel Cunard arrived in Scotland with plans for a UK to US mailboat service, Burns had put together a consortium within three weeks and raised £270,000, though interestingly using just £10,500 of his own. The profits from his mailboats were gradually buying out the other members of the consortium and leveraging the family fortune, allowing Burns to take on a glorious gothic starter castle, Castle Wemyss, on the Clyde outside Largs. However, by late 1854, the cash-cow mail business was threatened by the Earl of Eglinton's rival Ardrossan Line, which, with the Glasgow and South Western Railway Company, proposed a Parliamentary Bill to incorporate timetabling of rail and boats for faster delivery of passengers and mail to and from Ireland. George Burns had to sink that Bill if he was going to hang on to his contracts, which were so vital to his ambition. What he needed was insider information which could press all the right buttons for the politicians and the civil service.

Now I began to see why a millionaire businessman, not known for his artistic pursuits, offered hospitality to a middling-level English cash-strapped civil servant. I believe that Tony Trollope helped George Burns sink his rival's Bill by advising him on how to work the post office top brass and, through them, the politicians. Trollope certainly sang well for his supper. The Ardrossan Line petition was defeated and George Burns subsequently took it over; he also bought out the Cunard consortium. By the time Burns, Cunard and their Liverpool-based partner David McIver retired in the 1850s, their shares held outright were valued at £800,000. Later, when they raised private capital to become a joint stock company, the Cunard Steamship Company was valued at £2 million. It went public in 1880, to fund a massive expansion of the transatlantic business and the titanic battle with the White Star Line.

How many of us, like Trollope, would love the financial ease that such a cash cow brings? All too often, our professional success leads only to increasing want, and there is never, ever, enough money to satisfy our ego-driven needs. For Trollope, who painstakingly detailed his career earnings of £68,959 17s 5d, there was never enough money. There never would have been. Without spiritual values, there never is. For any of us.

Trollope always described his musings on his novels as 'castle building', and there is no doubt that life in the opulent Castle Wemyss provided Trollope with plenty of castle-building material, and this concerned God as well as Money. For the plot of *Barchester Towers* turns on ecclesiastical promotion and financial advancement in Barsetshire, with a new government promoting the evangelical wing of the Church of England. Academics have cited Trollope's extraordinary foresight in anticipating the arrival of Lord Palmerston's pro-evangelical administration. In fact, Trollope first learned about it at Castle Wemyss from one of George Burns' closest friends and most regular visitors, the fellow evangelical Lord Shaftesbury, Lord Palmerston's stepson and church adviser.

Published in 1857, *Barchester Towers* was Trollope's break-through novel; George Meredith writing in *The Westminster Review* called it, 'decidedly the cleverest novel of the season'. The concealment for over 140 years that the novel had been conceived and begun while its civil-servant author had been happily accepting hospitality from a leading government supplier with a problem, was cleverer still.

By 1870, once again, poor Tony Trollope was strapped for cash. He had resigned from the civil service. This struck me as out of character: with his level of financial insecurity, how could he forego a £500 per annum pension when he had just eight years to go? He had also been forced to sell his large home, through losing money fighting a by-election, and through his investment in the failing *St Paul's* magazine. His two sons also required serious amounts of money. Once again, the Burns family brought him luck – *The Eustace Diamonds*, partly written at Castle Wemyss, netted £2,500. Yet Trollope never alluded to Castle Wemyss in any writing about *The Eustace Diamonds*, even though there was now no need for concealment.

So what was the basis of this ongoing friendship between the novelist and ex-civil servant and this rich family? In 1878, Trollope joined the Burns family for a summer cruise to Iceland on HMS *Mastiff*. He wrote it up for his host, George Burns's son John, in a privately published account, titled *How the Mastiffs Went to Iceland*. John Burns's daughter Caroline, annotating *The World* article, writes: 'Anthony Trollope did write *How the Mastiffs Went to Iceland* and was much disgusted that no cheque resulted therefrom.'

Much disgusted? I bet he was. Trollope would have been only too aware of the pivotal role he had played in building their fortune. I think this remark tells us everything about the real basis of Tony Trollope's friendship with the Burns family. He had enjoyed a luxurious free holiday, and, as we know from his later grovelling letter to Burns, nice presents too – in a postscript he describes his wife 'flaunting' the gold buttons given to her. Yet so great was his financial need and, I would suggest, his habit of accepting cash from the Burns family, he let slip his disgust to his patron's daughter, who clearly does not hold him in the highest esteem.

The Burns family had the best of the bargain, as the financially powerful usually do. Documents in the Inverclyde Collection show that John Burns, in a shrewd marketing move, presented a copy of *How the Mastiffs Went To Iceland* to the Kaiser. Keen to cash in on Germany's economic and naval expansion, what better PR tool for the Chairman of a shipping line than a true story about the Burns family at sea, written by one of Britain's most famous and popular novelists? From long experience, I have learned that the business community never give houseroom to artists, unless they have something to offer. Trollope's currency was first the insider information, which secured the family fortune, followed by celebrity.

The Sunday Times bought my story[5] and I wrote it up for the *Trollopiana*, magazine of the Trollope Society, posting the findings on my website.[6] Professor Sir John Sutherland, the world-renowned Trollope scholar, welcomed my research, dubbing it 'The Trollope Bomb'. For me, Tony Trollope, whose stories are such masterpieces of financial fiction, now finally added up.

John Burns became the first Lord Inverclyde and, as one of the richest families in Britain, the Burnses entertained royalty and the international rich and famous for over a century, until the line died out in the 1950s. The roof was taken off Castle Wemyss, and by 1995 it was just a pile of rubble above the Clyde.

In an age where the financial power of global business controls so much of our lives, it is worth noting that on the World-wide Web, until my own website appeared, there was not one single mention of George and John Burns, whose fortunes were based on their own period's new mode of carrying information. Anthony Trollope, the jobsworth writer, on the other hand, who fretted about his personal spending, and so effectively used his commercial knowledge to ease the Burns family to such dazzling wealth, is fêted in thousands of pages throughout cyberspace.

The best literature teaches us to navigate through our own times, so Trollope's story can help us as ordinary investors as we count the cost of business double standards at the beginning of the millennium. For his long dealing with the Burns family and their cronies explains why Anthony Trollope, respectable civil servant in the postal service, a public-sector animal to his fingertips, was able to create such a monster and understand the nature of the evil genius of Augustus Melmotte, in *The Way We Live Now*, a title as contemporary as ever.

For in Melmotte, we see a fictional and fraudulent embodiment of so many of the technocrats, financiers and entrepreneurs of our own day, who at, or near, the height of the end of millennium boom, sold immensely overvalued companies or parcels of shares, often for nine-figure sums to the unsuspecting plcs, in which our own pensions were invested. Indeed, they make the Robber Barons look like small time spivs.

Yes, fact is so often stranger than fiction. For senior managers of our biggest insurance companies – so conservative in real life that they chose to train as actuaries during the swinging sixties – fully succumbed to the temptation of the siren calls of the equity cult. One could imagine feckless aristocrats falling for Melmotte's Mexican railway scam, but how extraordinary that, in our own day, some of the biggest culprits have been those employed by the mutual insurance companies, founded with such Victorian probity. Who would ever have imagined that these idealistic baby boomers would grow up to be so unaccountable to the rest of us?

The City knows exactly who today's Melmottes are, who schmoozed their way to getting out 'at the top' and inflicting an impecunious old age on millions of ordinary investors. J. K. Galbraith has called this the age of innocent fraud, but it is not innocent at all, just fraud within the law, with the modern Melmottes laughing all the way to the bank. Unlike Melmotte, who was disgraced, these individuals still grace the finest drawing rooms in the land – while landing the rest of us with debt in massively underfunded pension schemes, which will encumber economic growth and jobs for years to come.

So Who Profits from our Debt?

If the meticulous, high-earning Anthony Trollope could control neither his finances nor his financial insecurities, what hope is there for the rest of us, as we compete for resources on a far from even playing field?

Most of us are not in the Burns league; most of us are like Tony Trollope, wobbling our way through the month, robbing Peter to pay Paul. Yet if we are to try to make our spiritual values count, and bridge that gap between God and Money, we have to price its damage. Let's not buy the line that lifestyle debt is the norm for successful people; this is disinformation. Forget rubbish about 'new paradigms' too, that other buzz phrase much beloved of twenty-first-century snakeoil sales-men. We must remember that it was only back in the 1980s that people were supplicants in a mortgage queue, and con-sidered chequebooks rather racy, let alone credit cards.

Thanks to the magic of the fairy godmother market economy, as debt has been transformed into the sophisticated choice for successful professionals (i.e. anyone with a bank account), temptation is a norm. We are being a sold a line and when we bite, it is big business. Even when today's customer is supposedly empowered, what price progress when debt help-lines are swamped with desperate callers, and repossessions soar? Over 6 million UK households are having difficulty juggling monthly bills, and 9 million Britons are 'financial phobes', too traumatised to open bank statements or attend to their finances.[7] The human cost of debt in pain, lost hope, misery, broken relationships and lives is unimaginable. And this is in the respectable credit-worthy slice of the market.

But down at the 'sub prime lending' end of the scale, where lurk the loan sharks and doorstep lenders, lies the greatest human misery, which can blight generations. And it is big business. At present, according to the New Economics Foundation's latest debt report, 1.5 million people each week have debt-collectors knocking on their door for cash payments, with loan companies exacting payment of loans at 1000–2000 per cent interest on average borrowings of £940 in a sector worth £3.3 billion.[8] That Britain has a laissez-faire approach to predatory lending says much about the low priority such poor people have in government. Why is it easier to set up as a money-lender in the UK than it is to set up a credit union, which could effectively drive out the money-lenders who asset strip whole neighbourhoods?

Weaning ourselves off debt is probably as hard as giving up smoking, and requires us to break the spell of the marketing magic. Smokers are often advised to deprive themselves of the comforting ritual of the cigarette packet, with its solid shape and shiny paper, and, instead, are advised to keep cigarettes in a plastic bag. Another ploy is aversion therapy: a clear plastic bag full of stinking cigarette stubs that they can breathe in. So perhaps we debtors should start labelling debt not as credit, but as usury, and our creditors as usurers, in order to begin feeling a similar degree of useful nausea. Let us start giving debt back its old stigma.

In the *Divine Comedy*, Dante portrays the usurers, or the money-lenders, as anti-social, he puts them down in the seventh circle of the Inferno, sitting on burning sands with cashboxes around their necks, condemned for being violent towards others. Jesus marked both the beginning and end of his ministry by demonstrating his robust opinion of usurious financial services, by kicking over the money-changers' tables in the Temple. Yes, they were different times, but, as the case of Anthony Trollope shows, human nature never changes: the world is always divided into buyers and sellers, exploiters and exploited. So which are we? And are we being cut off from our history of fearing debt, to suit other people?

Our ancestors, living through wars, famines and hardship, would have seen debt very differently from us. Viewed through a Judaeo-Christian prism, they would have known that throughout the Bible debt equals slavery. A message rammed home week after week in the pulpit. 'Our money is all spent . . . There is nothing left . . . Buy us and our land in exchange for food. We with our land will become slaves to Pharaoh . . .' (Genesis 47:18–19). Dramatic words as, hungry and broke, the Egyptians plead with Pharaoh's chief accountant, who had successfully predicted the boom and the bust. We shall be your slaves, they say, in return for food. How low can you go?

This attitude to debt has disappeared in a secular age. Yet the Protestant work ethic, that key ingredient of the Industrial Revolution, which believed that hard work was necessary for redemption, remains firmly in place – the consequences of which we shall discuss in the next chapter. Why? Perhaps because this nugget of Christian thought is such a very useful creed for an economic system, predicated on a population working to service the very different redemption of financial debt.

Perhaps it is time for a new look at an old-fashioned word, 'Redemption'.

Case Study 2: View from a Pawnbroker[9]

It is a hot sunny Tuesday afternoon in August. Everyone else is off to the beach, but I have a column to fill, so I am in Glasgow, spending a day behind the counter of a city-centre pawnbroker.

How strange in an age when debt is so desirable, that taboos about the 3,000-year-old profession of the pawnbroker remain so embedded in the DNA of middle-class respectability. These taboos do not prevent business booming, however, which is up 200 per cent in a year; staff remind me that the previous month was a five-week month, when your average punter had the mortgage and holidays to pay for, plus loss of income while on holiday if he or she were self-employed. VAT and income tax are due. Perspiring professionals scurry into the shop looking harassed; business people are pledging stock, which can be redeemed later in the year. It is cheaper borrowing from pawnbrokers than from doorstep credit, but the APRs are still swingeing, averaging from 40 per cent to 85 per cent – not a bad margin for a low- risk business, where the owner can always sell the goods if clients don't come back.

On another side of the building, unredeemed pledges are sold at 50 per cent below retail price. Here, eternity rings, testament to the impermanence of true love, are piled high, along with bracelets and sapphire rings. Round the back, staff open huge heavy safe doors to show me trays upon trays of jewellery, neatly packed and labelled in small plastic bags, representing tens of thousands of current pledges. Beautiful works of art are stacked for auction, unclaimed. The staff always enjoy something special: a Fabergé Box and a Russell Flint painting came in recently. They are expert in the subtleties of human psychology; with married couples, the wife's jewellery is always pawned last, though the husband's car is always redeemed first.

I stand behind the wooden booths, which are built like confessionals to house the constant stream of customers. Depression seems to have been branded into the panelling. I see an old woman miserably rip off jewellery, her face full of pain; next door, a smartly dressed young man peels off his Rolex with élan; it has diamond numbers, he explains, so it must be good for a grand. Everywhere is the sweet stench of anxiety and humiliation. Only once, amid the tense muttering, do I hear laughter. In one booth, a woman is flashing her engagement ring, just redeemed by her husband. As she turns her head to say good bye, the electricity in her smile could light up a small town. The door bangs behind them. The clerk picks up the pledge sheet and tears it up. 'The pledge's now been redeemed,' he explains to me. 'It's finished.'

It is finished. Only then, finally, standing there looking at the bits of the pledge sheet, half-fallen on the floor under the booth, half in the wastepaper bin, do I understand for the first time what Redemption really means. Jesus, a creative with such power over words, must have known that only a financial term like this would ever be strong enough to get through our thick skulls and make us realise what he could do for us. How clever. For whatever the ancient connotations of Redemption in the Jewish faith, Jesus played over the heads of the Jewish establishment to an international audience, and needed an international language: money. Only the term 'Redemption', so perfectly understood by anyone who has ever been worried sick about debt – almost all of us – could make us begin to understand what his payment meant.

Redemption. His death on the cross pays off our sins – our debts in Church of Scotland parlance – cancels our pledge and wipes the slate clean. What an extraordinary compliment. What an incentive to make a fresh start.

What a waste. This word 'Redemption' has lost its power to shock in the English-speaking world, for our language has been distorted over decades, in a relentless drive to grow market share for financial institutions. And so successful has this been that debt has been transformed into credit. And so we now have no image in our collective imagination of a slate being wiped clean, because being in debt all our adult lives is, to our credit, a norm, nothing wrong with it. Well done, we're now paid-up members of the human race. (Oh, by the way Mr Brown, have you seen our special remortgage deal for long-standing customers?)

If language expresses the way we see our world, we are poor indeed.

So, What is the True Price of Debt?

So let us stop kidding ourselves. We are not 'masters of the universe', to use Tom Wolfe's magical phrase. We are fragile. It only takes a big piece of spending, or a sudden change of circumstances to tip us into unsustainable debt. Keith Tondeur runs Credit Action Line, a Christian charity debt helpline which, with associate organisations, counsels 150,000 people in the UK a year.[10] When I ring, Keith has just been advising a vicar with unsecured debts of over £110,000. A depressingly common experience apparently, there are several new cases every week of six-figure debt burdens.

'Usually people take on the debt they feel they can pay, but it only takes illness, unemployment, an interest rise or a property slump and, suddenly, it is unsustainable. If you borrow £30K or £40K, you are paying £250–£500 a month. This soon rolls up and soon it is £60K–£70K, which means the interest is now £500–£1,000 a month. Then the only solution is for a relative to step forward to pay up a proportion and ask for the rest to be written off, or bankruptcy.'

The consequences of debt are evils any self-respecting devil could wish for: arguments leading to domestic violence against spouses and children, family breakdown, poverty, distrust, loss of honesty and friendship. They could happen to any of us.

Let me tell you about Jimmy. I was told about him when I started writing the ethical money column for the *Big Issue* Scotland. How many of us take the trouble to look into the eyes of the homeless people selling this magazine, who stand shivering at street corners, let alone ever consider that they maybe once had mortgages, pensions, pin numbers, credit cards? Nor imagine just what huge odds they are fighting: it takes only three weeks of sleeping rough for lasting psychological damage.

Jimmy ran a successful plumbing business in Glasgow employing twenty men. Jimmy had a big, flash car, and a posh house in a well-to-do suburb, a wife and two kids. A committed Rotarian, a regular at Chamber of Commerce business breakfasts, he was well known for always being upbeat and doing anyone a good turn. Cashflow was sometimes a bit touch and go, but when isn't it when running a business? Then, in 1994, after years of stress, servicing debts at 15 per cent interest rates and dealing with late payers – some of them large companies with annual reports dripping with corporate social responsibility policies – his marriage fell apart. Distraught, Jimmy took his eye off the ball at work, and the business and personal debts mounted, until he had £10,000 in credit-card debts – peanuts today, when graduates face leaving university with three times more debt. He divorced and, by 1996, after exhausting all lines of credit and good will, he was living on the street selling the *Big Issue*. He sold it for two years before the cold got him. The average age of death in Scotland for homeless men is just forty-eight, below some third-world countries. He died in 1998, having lost contact with his children.

His name isn't Jimmy; I've changed it. But he was a real person. I have told Jimmy's story to some senior financial services professionals, who have been amazed, never having associated *Big Issue* vendors with people like themselves before, nor ever thought of them as former customers.

We need to connect now. For what a loss of potential to the economy Jimmy represents. I shall be discussing some of the real causes of homelessness, but let us at least acknowledge that homelessness comes at the end of a not very long, debt-driven continuum; and that we are all impoverished by each other's debts, in ways we dare not imagine. I meet a social worker at a party. 'Only a blink of time separates many of us from Armageddon because of debt,' she tells me. 'You can usually trace events right back to a bad debt or a piece of unaffordable spending, which then snowballs. Just one.'

I am in a public library holding a money workshop for around thirty members of the general public. I have just told the audience the story of Jimmy, and they are struck that his decline took only four years. We discuss the huge amount of junk mail all of us receive daily on our doormats and online. It takes only one sucker to make it pay. I ask everyone to make a pie diagram of his or her own life and divide it up into health, relationships, employment, housing and friends. Just how resilient are we to a financial reverse? Once we have done this, we all realise that debt, even in quite small amounts, radically cripples our ability to fight adversity in every area. A young woman comes over and asks me for advice. That morning she has just received £5,000 directly into her bank account, it was a loan from a company she had approached for just £500. I can see the fear in her eyes that the £5,000 will easily be spent. I tell her to pay it back, not to use it – it is not worth it. It is in the finance company's interest if she loses her peace of mind. I tell her about the day I went into the building society, yes a building society, to tell them, that after years of living like the proverbial church mouse, my husband and I were paying off our mortgage. 'What do you mean you're paying off your mortgage?' The expression on the face of the woman behind the counter did not speak of congratulation, but cold fury. Two had got away. This is why our forebears thought of usury as anti-social.

In the papers, a couple of stories about debt catch my eye. There is an amusing story of a New Yorker, Karyn Bosnak, who, finding herself $20,000 in debt and unemployed, set up a website (www.savekaryn.com) calling for visitors to give generously and make the world a better place. Within a few weeks she had cleared half her debts and was inundated with job offers. A rare good news story, and I enjoy her site for its upbeat derring-do. Yet I prefer the integrity of a story from Taiwan, about a businesswoman left by a crooked associate with a US $ 500,000 debt, who worked sixteen hours a day for five years running an iced snack business in steamy Taipei until she redeemed the debt. How huge the temptation must have been to have gone bankrupt and let society pick up the debt?

Now, in the UK and other Western nations, we like to think that our country will never go bankrupt like, say, a country such as Argentina, where middle-class professionals flog wedding rings and furniture to buy food, as dollar savings shrink into pesos and cash is rationed. Our state is not like that, is it? No, it is not. The state of Argentina went bankrupt for $140 billion, whereas in the UK debt lies less on the state than on the backs of the people; we stagger like beasts of burden under the weight of £850 billion of personal debt. And rising.

Some of it is self-inflicted, though our tax burden is among the heaviest in the developed world, but the effect, as we bend our noses to the grindstone under the weight of this, is that we're keeping the economy moving nicely. Consumers admit to market researchers that they are more insecure about spending, but they keep on spending. But as a cynical market analyst in the City remarked in a newspaper interview, 'What does it matter if people aren't smiling as they spend, as long as they're still spending!'

So let us ask once more: who else profits from our indebtedness? Isn't it, for example, terribly convenient for the state, because it keeps us quiet, nose to the grindstone, in the twenty-first-century equivalent of domestic service? Politicians are not going to worry about rioting students, not when students have £20,000 of debt on their heads. As for the rest of the debt-ridden working population, who stay sane only by contemplating the equity in their houses, we are hardly likely to spend too much energy questioning any democratic deficit in our governing institutions, are we? And what about the truly poor, who are slaves to the loan sharks? One can imagine the average Whitehall Mandarin who knows the Bible easily writing them off – well the poor are always with us, aren't they? They can't afford to say boo.

Employers also benefit from our debt. They know we are hardly going to rock the boat with a mortgage to pay. I often wonder when reading articles in the human resources press, whether our endemic culture of office bullying is, at heart, debt-driven because the bullies know that fellow employees have to take it, because, with the mortgage due at the end of the month, they are not free to walk out. So let's list those who find our debt convenient for the balance of power. Sellers of debt (the financial services institutions, at whatever end of the scale), owners of debt-free assets, the state and employers. Quite a list.

Do we all have to fall so obediently into line, robbed of our freedom and our creativity and time with our families? Can't we start asking awkward questions, refusing to go meekly under the yoke? And if our debt is to fund our high standard of living, are all these possessions cluttering up our homes really worth such a high price? Can't we try a new low-debt way of living, if only for no other reason, just to see how rich it would make us feel?

For if we do not, where do we go from here? I look at my audience in this Edinburgh church hall, who are clearly suffering from the 50 per cent stock-market falls, and suggest that debt has brought their children's generation to the edge of a financial abyss. I don't want to sound overdramatic, but I do believe that there is a reckoning for all of us who, as the *fin de siècle* stock-market boomed, used debt to buy lifestyle and shares, believing that the markets would rise ever upwards and float us out of the need to live within our means. Houses turned into piggy banks, to be raided on a regular basis, and we thought market economics would supply our standard of living and the basic laws of money management no longer applied us. Like Trollope, we lost the plot.

This is not some piece of hindsight virtue. Rather chillingly given subsequent events in New York, I wrote on 9 November 1997, in *Scotland on Sunday*:

> My gut feel is that something is going to wipe the smug grins off of those pasty-faced baby boomers spinning their self-satisfied, 'I guess two o'clock will be a good time to buy the market' line. What an interesting sight it will be when these people, with their identical backgrounds, education and life-style, finally stampede for the exit at the same time. If and when that happens, Wall Street will come tumbling down, and stay down, faster than a dynamited sky-rise.
>
> The truth is that neither the bulls nor the bears really know what is going to happen. Or when. Every time mankind thinks he has found a new paradigm – in our case high sustainable growth in a low inflationary environment – the ancient rules reassert themselves. So will the Bible's seven years of plenty (for which read Alan Greenspan's six and a half years of business expansion) be followed by seven years of famine?

I concluded that we were witnessing what I dubbed 'The Greenspan Bubble – a handy label picked up on most memorably a few months later in the *Economist* cover story: 'Alan in Bubbleland.'

Six years on since I wrote that article, with experienced City pundits calling the equity cult train crash the worst since the 1930s and the investment community's mantra of 'Invest for the long term and never disinvest' having given way to 'Nobody could have predicted this', the financial markets and the geopolitical landscape have changed out of all recognition to the absurdly self-pitying whine of 1999. But the real economic pain is yet to kick in, as business gets to grips with the pressing need to shed jobs to restore profitability, pension funds and dividend yields and so attract investors back.

In the late 1990s' boom the central authorities effectively rigged the markets after the near collapse in the UK of the Long Term Capital Management hedge fund, and kept on doing so as each successive crisis (including 9/11) hit. While old City hands long retired from the Square Mile spoke sagely to me in hushed tones that equities were heading for 'the mother of all baths' (a City expression meaning to lose one's shirt) and would probably take the housing market with them, the hedonistic party carried on long after the punch bowl should have been taken away. Happy in his brief that the bursting of asset bubbles was not in his job description, Greenspan presided over the investment orgy as we rushed into the market grabbing as much as we could with both hands, like children into a sweetie shop.

Sadly, it may be several years before we fully and finally comprehend the legacy of our generation's greed and collective folly. Furthermore, even the most powerful stock market rally will be vulnerable to equally powerful setbacks, such is the new fragility of faith in artificially inflated markets. Finally, no one can really predict how bad the housing train crash is going to be, or when and at what level it will happen.

Now that is the big-picture money, but what about lower down the scale far from the FTSE Index, where debt-driven poverty lurks? Frankly, I believe that churches of all denominations have a huge opportunity to prove their relevance to the rest of us, as the market economy curdles, on both. First, in calling for greater probity in business, reclaiming and celebrating nationally the business heritage of Britain's devout Quaker dynasties, who built ground-breaking businesses in the nineteenth century. And then by lobbying government at the highest level for far tighter consumer protection to stamp out predatory lending, such as a legal interest rate ceiling as exists in Germany, and the abolition of domestic bailiffs; by investing heavily in services offering debt counselling, financial education and budgeting advice.

Down at the harsh end of the debt culture, Church Action on Poverty[11] has been doing sterling work for years, banging government and policy advisers' heads together, not least with their innovative Debt on the Doorstep campaign. Yet it still seems extraordinary to me, a layperson, that their work appears to be considered by Christians in the UK as somehow just another good cause among many when, instead, their campaigns should lie at the very heart of every congregation and every church-office operation. For what is Christianity for, if it is not about fighting poverty? What is the point of having God in our lives if we cannot help others, not least with money?

Why can't we have high-profile, cleverly marketed church credit unions attached to every area, just as we have church schools? Churches could co-operate across denominations, aggressively marketing Jesus' radical message of stewardship, with as much energy and chutzpah as the debt sellers; they could take on the market economy with God's messages about debt, which the Bible could not spell out more clearly. And why not join with other faiths to create market share, and really give the financial services industry a run for its money?

Why are we taking so long? Perhaps it is the blame culture which attaches itself to the poor, that half-hidden nuance that they are, in some *My Fair Lady* sense, undeserving. Over the years, anti-poverty campaigners have told me that they find an extraordinary lack of urgency among some church officials who control the purse strings and run the church. Safe in the middle class, they are apparently unable to imagine what it is like to be on the wrong side of the door when the bailiff knocks. How much nicer and exotic it is to campaign against international debt – which affects poor people safely tucked away on some other continent – than it is to campaign for bread-and-butter legislation changes, to help the poor in the local housing estate down the road?

We cannot afford this. Christians must lay down a gauntlet to the professionals who handle church assets or run the parishes to bridge that gap between God and Money and call them to account. For if our churches fail to take a lead, because they have become so corporate that the main deal is tip-toeing round financiers and financial institutions to keep the cash flowing, then they are no better than all the other landed and vested interests, which have a clear stake in keeping the little people in bondage.

Christianity was founded by a wonderful radical, who turned over the tables of the money-changers, but church leaders today might ask themselves whether the ship has hit the rocks on their watch.

4

$£$£$£$£$£$£$£$£

THE HIGH PRICE OF A LOUSY WORK–LIFE BALANCE

F OR me, the realisation that my work–life balance was so bad, and that I was rapidly heading for a premature demise, came one London summer evening in 1995. I had just walked back from the Underground station into my road and was now sitting on the pavement outside my house in a business suit, feet in the gutter, briefcase propped up against a neighbour's wall. I sat there, *Waiting for Godot*-style, for over half an hour, unable to stand up and go in the front door. Inside were two small children who had not seen their parents all day. My brain said I had to go in, do baths, homework, cuddles. But my body just remained on the pavement, the clock ticking by on babysitter time, dreading the moment when I would have to turn into a pumpkin parent, the moment when the local church clock struck 7 p.m. Much as I loved my children, I could not cope; I was too tired. All I really wanted in the whole world was a large glass of wine. Preferably two. Or three.

Not clever. That day I had just received a brilliant assessment at work, I had been promised a pay rise, praised for my performance. Wasn't I lucky to be in such a privileged position? Of course I was. I was an asset to my organisation, a valuable piece of human capital contributing to a vibrant brand. Any deficit in this comfortable and lucrative financial exchange of labour and salary was being paid by my children, because miracle worker though I was, I lacked the ability to be in two places at once. I was 'having it all': career, kids, home, happy marriage, yet inside I felt I had nothing at all. Lots of women will know this feeling. I remember a one-liner I once wrote in an article on working mothers. 'A mother's place is in the red and in the wrong.' Very droll.

How much space do we have during our working lives to process where we are going, what we are doing? Or are we so busy keeping all those plates spinning, we dare not look around us to see what we are becoming?

Often, the realisation that we have a lousy work–life balance comes when there is a crisis, when we are finally forced to wake up, when we realise just how much our lives are damaged by TATT – being tired all the time – that ague of the mind, body and spirit which never leaves even after a main summer holiday, when we return to the office feeling just enough rested to know how exhausted we are.

Yet it is difficult to work on a good work–life balance when there is so much unemployment around, when we need so much money just to service our lives. As we rush around overdrawn at the energy bank, are we suiting ourselves or our bosses, bank managers, financial service providers and friends, who like us for the jobs we do, or the kind of lifestyle we can buy into?

It cannot be sustainable. So why do we listen to our bodies only when they are beginning to break down, or to the people who love us most only when we are past the last chance? Because of money, I would suggest. As well as relatively recent cultural norms. We may find ourselves paying other high prices for a bad work–life balance, too, which could include lost reputation and financial peace of mind. We make mistakes, take short cuts, overspend, let people and influences into our lives, because we are too busy to vet or question, or apply the usual filters. Too late we count the cost, only as all those spinning plates crash.

As I have been writing this, the tabloid press has been full of so-called 'Cheriegate', the story of how UK Prime Minister

Tony Blair's wife used the services of a convicted conman Peter Foster to buy two flats in Bristol, one for her eldest son and the other for rental income. Throw in a lifestyle guru fitness instructor/paid best friend who was an ex-porn actress, tales of New Age pendants and nude scrub downs, and a classic newspaper sting, set against a fire-fighters' strike and rows over university top-up fees, and here we have all the ingredients for a feeding frenzy of media self-righteousness with a Number 10 Downing Street press office in panic mode. As the Hydra-headed rumours proliferate, the reputation of Cherie Blair, the Prime Minister's clever hard-working wife, is permanently damaged. She tearfully appears on television to give a statement, all sackcloth and ashes, credibility in shreds.

How could she have used a convicted conman bound for deportation, whom she had apparently never met, to secure a discount on the flats? Did she give him legal advice about fighting deportation? Who lied, who failed to come clean? Why did this QC not immediately sort out this situation when the conman said that his company would pick up her accountancy bill? Follow the money! No one did anything illegal, yet there is no doubt that the political and career consequences are messy.

Yet take away the media circus and this is just a classic case of a poor work–life balance. Busy, stressed-out super-women combining high-powered work, family and public life are so 'up to high doh', to use a great Scots expression, that they have no time to think; stressed out, they use gyms and meet – in leotards and therefore feeling vulnerable – people they never would normally encounter in a million years, who scrape an acquaintance and then move in on their lives. Diana, Princess of Wales, was another prime target. Life for such women rolls on in an inspired muddle, for there is no time or space to process what life is doing to them.

Usually it takes a catalyst to create a crisis. In Cherie Blair's case, it was her first child leaving home to go to university. Such an event hits working mothers hard; it can seem like a bereavement for a missed childhood, for we only ever have a short leasehold on our children's lives. So Cherie Blair, perhaps finding it hard to let go, looks to buy two flats in the university town, but, too busy to look or negotiate, buys in hired help in unknown quantities. During the TV statement the Prime Minister's wife's voice broke when she referred to her son's first term away at university. But into the crusher of this stressed-out, well-meaning, clever maelstrom of a life go these mistakes and a damaged reputation for public consumption. One cannot begin to imagine the emotional cost.

Nevertheless, Mrs Blair is a star role model for women. Classic cash-rich, time-poor material, and therefore positioned in our aspirational culture as having it all. Career, husband and children.

Cash rich, time poor. In these uncertain times, perhaps we need to rethink the message in this description. Surely the term 'cash rich, time poor' does not describe wealth? One source of wealth cannot cancel out another source of poverty. It is like being rich in food, but poor in water. We may enjoy a banquet but, as our lips crack, we're still living on borrowed time. Time poverty, I suggest, is the real poverty in the rich industrialised West. Our high standard of living has indeed been won, but at a price to ourselves and our families.

Of course we all need money for food and shelter, and we like money too, for the freedom it brings, but if we are considering wealth, then there is a difference between wealth in time and wealth in money. Time to be with our families and to grow as human beings has to be more precious than money, for it is non-negotiable. We might live on hope and baked beans for years with time and space for our families, but there is always the chance we can acquire money, given a bit of luck. But none of us, however rich, can never, ever, earn, win, barter, borrow or steal back time. And our money wealth can disappear before our eyes if the stock market falls. Therefore, the absence of time as an item on our personal balance sheet is more than an omission, it is an aberration we cannot afford.

So how rich are we? How poverty stricken are we made by our working culture in the West? Not just women, but men, too, would love more time to be with their children. We are brainwashed and bamboozled into thinking a lousy life–work balance is virtuous and will make us rich, when it is in fact draining us of resources and lifeblood every day. While others, as we shall see in the next chapter, become effortlessly rich.

One fiction we spin ourselves is that our present living hell is only temporary – of course we'll have a fine time when we retire, then we'll have time to spend with our grandchildren, even if we have barely seen our own children. As if our bodies will never suffer the consequences of our excess; as if we shall have any pensions by the time the financial services industry has finished investing our money; as if our children will want to reproduce on cue anyway. One in four men now work more than 50 hours a week, while a survey in May 2002 by London head-hunters Joslin Rowe[1] revealed half the fathers they interviewed spend less than five minutes a day with their children.

Yet our present time poverty here in the West is a relatively recent phenomenon. When I say we, I mean the 20 per cent of the global workforce who have the mobility, education and resources to kill themselves with overconsumption and over-work. In the UK, our medieval ancestors enjoyed far more feast days, saints' days and days of rest. Time off work meant more time for family life, and allowed the growth of community bonds, which were sorely needed in hard times. Life was short, but potentially merry between wars. It has only been since the Industrial Revolution that work has predominated at all income levels, with free time for play or study relegated to the margins of life not spent working or sleeping.

But in the last twenty years of market-economy reforms, there has been a quantum leap, reaching the point, according to the Work Life Balance Trust,[2] that 80 per cent of our visits to UK doctors are stress related, with the annual National Health Service bill for stress-induced ill-health running at £2 billion. Absenteeism now costs UK industry £5 billion per annum with 7 million workdays lost to stress-related illness. In a survey released in February 2003 by the Work Foundation,[3] absentee levels were found to have shot up to over 4 per cent in 2002 across Britain, up from 2.9 per cent in 2001, the highest since they were first monitored in 1996. Twelve million of us are on anti-depressants to block out the pain. The International Labour Office[4] suggests that, in the EU as a whole, one in ten workers is suffering from depression, anxiety, stress or burn out, with spending on mental-health problems potentially 3–4 per cent of gross domestic product. This is big money. So, like pollution, are these health bills just another item of the real cost of doing business and maximising profits, which is dumped on to the wider community? When are we going to start adding up the real sum?

One problem of a bad work–life balance twenty-first-century style is that the life bit of the equation, pushed to the margins of weekends and late evenings, becomes a shortened, expensive, and often debt-driven muddle, possible only with huge amounts of expensive, bought-in solutions. Just as we are too tired to think about our lives and the values we have, so we are usually too tired to find out just where we are financially. And this exacerbates our problems. In fact, it seems to be a rule that the more successful we are, the greater the paperwork disorder in our private life. Many people I know well and respect, who happily handle millions for clients, point shamefaced at plastic bags or dusty files under their bed or above the ironing board, where household bills and accounts are kept, along with barely glanced bank statements. I bet the Blairs upstairs in the flat at Number 11 Downing Street, with four children to contain, have been no different than any of us. So high flyers may impress with their fancy computer programs for their share portfolios, but they rarely have a handle on household accounts, that messy spending which accounts for those novel-length monthly bank statements.

However professional and slick the impression we make to the outside world, our work–life balance always tips in favour of our employers and clients, rather than ourselves. Hence the reason why so much of our hard-earned money is wasted each week in buying what we already have, but haven't the time to find, and why our personal mess mountain grows. I call it the shoe-polish syndrome. When I finally took a grip of my lousy work–life balance, I found I had ten tins of black shoe polish under the kitchen sink, because it was easier to buy another one on the way to work than stop to look. This is a small indication of the gigantic waste of money that can happen when we have a badly balanced lifestyle.

Now is the time to restore some order. For as we live longer and learn to nourish portfolio careers, we must be assertive in our management of our money and our time. No one else is going to look out for us if we don't.

Let us estimate how much holding down our working life actually costs – in transport, bought-in help, clothes, convenience foods, domestic help, gardening, childcare and not forgetting alcohol as a relaxant. Let's consider other costs, in lost social capital, that non-financial wealth which makes life worth living – parenting time, voluntary work, building friendships, networks, learning new skills, support structures, a faith, serving others' needs – plus that other huge source of wealth, good health. If the cost in lost social capital is low and health is good, then we clearly have a good work–life balance. But if the debit side is looking heavy, then we must consider the total cost and ask ourselves whether we are in fact working at a thumping loss.

Of course, in justification of our long working days, we may argue that office networks give us all the support that we need. Concierge services (personal or domestic services) are booming. But we are talking life here, not just our present work. In some working environments, we may suddenly become a non-person to people we have spent years working with, the moment we hand in our security pass.

The key word is balance. If the imbalance is too much in favour of work, then we must start setting a limit to the underlying cost. Particularly given current job insecurity, and also pensions, which, for many, are not going to deliver what our elders have enjoyed.

That evening, as I sat on that suburban London pavement, if you had asked me about my life, I would have said my husband and I were success stories. We were earning high City salaries but, the following New Year, with both our offices closed for the holidays, we sat down and started adding up the costs. Horrified, we saw the extent of the damage, and that our high standard of living was unsustainable. The high joint income was not worth the stress, expenses and appalling cost to family life; the toll was rapidly taking twenty years off our natural lifespan. It was hard to change, but we started making plans about how we could get by with less money, and carve out another working life: rediscovering our creativity and our very souls.

So often I read obituaries of senior business people who die in middle age always 'after a long illness', comparatively young and leaving behind all the toys. How many of us would trade an extra year with our family, let alone an extra thirty? Is driven business ambition just a subtle form of mental illness, which puts selfish compulsions before a well-balanced life? Or is it a failure to imagine a bigger picture?

One useful exercise is to work out how much the household has earned over the past six years, then put down ballpark annual outgoings and estimate whether our lifestyle has gone up disproportionately to income. This is particularly useful to the self-employed and small business people, though it could help anyone in a 'proper job' prone to flash the plastic. For the truth is, as we rush around turbo-driven with plans and projects, many of us manage the interesting trick of living on air, on the basis of our last good year – rather than our average yearly income. We may continue to live a prosperous executive lifestyle, with foreign holidays, new kitchens and expensive cars, but the difference is made up, as if we didn't know, not from air, but start-up loans, credit cards or remortgages from our piggy-bank houses. As a result, lots of very hard-working, small-business people end up, after ten years, more in debt than when they started.

Life is too precious to live in an expensive muddle, being driven by exterior forces and cultural norms that we have no time or space to comprehend fully. We are worth more to God than sparrows, we are not merely the sum of what we consume, so let us work hard, but not necessary at work, to get a life.

What about the Workers?

The phrase 'work–life balance', as illustrated in the media, tends to conjure up a certain well-paid, well-heeled aspirational image. The subtext: I am simply *soooo* busy and in demand, making space is *such* a challenge!

But what about the poor, or the nearly poor? Don't they deserve a work–life balance too? Are they not of equal worth? They have an even greater challenge in their bit of the free-market economy for, here, fear rules. Acres of EU workplace rules and regulations may exist, but no one has the courage to insist on them. This world is brought to life by *Guardian* journalist Fran Abrams in her remarkable book *Below the Breadline: Living on the Minimum Wage*,[5] which describes three months she spent working for the minimum wage as a cleaner at the Savoy Hotel in London, on a bottling line in a Yorkshire factory and as an assistant in an Aberdeen old people's home. Here, she meets desperate, gritty people living on bags of pasta and stale bread. People who shoulder fourteen-hour days, too scared to complain, and work through illness and petty injustices, designed to slice pennies off the payroll.

> If people were houses, the characters in this book would be parked on some 1960s outer ring estate, ignored and forgotten. They lack the grubby inner city allure of those at the very bottom of the heap. The homeless. The addicts. The refugees. And so, when the latest anti-poverty spoils are passed around, they probably aren't even there. They're at work, or standing at a bus stop somewhere with their shopping bags. Thinking it isn't about them . . . But even dingy semis on outer-ring estates can have sunflowers growing in their gardens. They can, if it is the season for it, be ablaze with Christmas lights. They can have outrageous scarlet painted doors or multi-coloured stone

cladding. Just because you've got the imprint of someone else's boot on your forehead, it doesn't mean you're boring. It doesn't mean you never have any fun. You just have to work harder at it, that's all.

In such an environment, when we are all, more or less, cost centres, to be cut if a cheaper option comes along, it is very hard to think we are worth more than the lilies of the field. What a joke to think in terms of a work–life balance in such conditions.

Yet it is precisely because so many of us are pawns of the market economy, whether toiling in an air-conditioned office or on a factory line, that we owe it to ourselves to do some creative lateral thinking to ensure our own survival. God has to be allowed into this money-making equation somewhere, otherwise working along this continuum, human beings are reduced to the status of Victorian pit ponies. Are we supposed to work until we keel over in the street, to be carried away with the rubbish?

As I suggested in the last chapter, the Protestant work ethic, which so brilliantly propelled the Industrial Revolution, apparently has much to answer for. Yet if we read *Self-Help*, Samuel Smiles' business book smash hit of the 1850s, we can see what an alluring upbeat, can-do spirit his ideas had; no wonder they connected so well to a mass-reading public; no wonder his creed created so many business empires. 'There is no discredit but honour, in every right walk of industry, whether it be in tilling the ground, making tools weaving fabric or selling products behind the counter.'[6]

Gone is the idea of passive acceptance of salvation from the traditional Catholic perspective, the idea of the 'salvation economy' was to build Jerusalem now. Gone, too, was the pastoral idyll of the countryside as cultural icon. Well, until you made your pile and could play country gentleman. Now satanic mills offered nothing less than a salvation economy. All was possible with 'the spirit of self help', which would pull the aspiring working classes up by their teetotaller boot-straps.

But then, this Protestant work ethic was not about selfish individualism, but was placed within a community framework, supported by the social cohesion of extended family and community obligations, working to commonly accepted values. As Richard Donkin outlines in his wonderful book *Blood, Sweat and Tears: The Evolution of Work*,[7] the most successful practitioners of this ethic were the Quakers, who, barred from universities, professions, church and army, went into ironworks, chemicals and confectionery, bridging the gap between God and unrighteous Mammon with hard work, good service and entrepreneurship. The rest of society appreciated their trust, loyalty and honesty; their commitment to the customer broke the complacency of the old trade guild closed shops. In the UK, it was companies such as Lloyds of Birmingham (iron manufacturers) who offered lines of credit to customers. David Barclay's bank, and confectioners such as Fry, Cadbury and Rowntree, also led the way. Exported to the States, the new Promised Land, this Quaker style, unhindered by the old feudal establishment, succeeded brilliantly. 'All true work is religion,' wrote Thomas Carlyle. Amen to that, if it delivered the American dream.

The Protestant work ethic went through various guises, from the practical philanthropy at the New Lanark Mills, where Quakers backed social entrepreneur Robert Owen, accepting a 5 per cent return on their money rather than a possible 15 per cent, in order for schools to be built in place of mills for child workers. 'I know that society may be formed so as to exist without poverty, with health greatly improved, with little if any misery, and with intelligence and happiness increased a hundred fold,' Owen wrote.[8]

Though this did not widely catch on, it was a benchmark. By 1895, Quaker George Cadbury was measuring out the land at Bourneville for workers' housing, calculating one-sixth of an acre per house with six fruit trees per worker. He had the vision to see that this sustainable community would in time boast a doctor's surgery, schools, clubhouses and a sports pavilion.

However, in the 1930s there came a less philanthropic twist, with Frederick Taylor's 'scientific management', the invention of time and motion studies, of cost–benefit analyses, which saw creativity and potential wasted in the interests of efficiency. This was taken to extremes and distorted by the Nazis in the mass extinction of the Jews, gypsies and homosexuals. *Arbeit macht frei* was written on the gates of Auschwitz. Work makes you free was the lie, when death alone was on offer.

In the 1950s and 1960s, the ethic redeveloped into the age of management, where creativity and potential were merely allowed in the management classes. Mimicking the 'officers and men' social order of the forces and the British establishment, it bred inefficiency and decline, as strikes and confrontations in the 1970s proliferated. Then once again, in the 1980s, the Protestant work ethic was re engineered into market economics for grown-ups. If you kept your job. Working life was delayered and downsized by management consultants talking of 'empowerment' of the workforce and 'unlocking creativity', principally because it was cheap and cut costs. So the workforce, exhausted and overworked, did three jobs at once without a secretary, thanks to new technology. But the goodies on offer that we could buy with our hard-earned money didn't seem to make us happy.

How extraordinary in an increasingly secular world to see how this fundamentalist Christian creed should survive so beautifully, even among driven professionals who would not be seen dead in a church. But the creed by now had been redesigned with the core of community cohesion hollowed out, ambition replaced loyalty, debt and consumption replaced Smiles' thrift. Heresy is to admit we'd rather have the luxury of time, less responsibility and stress if we are under fifty. What do you mean you want to leave at six o'clock to see your children before they go to bed? The well-worn line that in the UK people work the longest hours in Europe has a comforting nuance that others are continental slackers! In the 1990s, spending more time with your family became a postmodern ironic euphemism for professional failure.

Sir Charles Handy's famous formula was indeed the key to boosting shareholder value in the 1980s. Half the people were paid twice as much to produce three times more – the lucky few were told by doctors that their stress-related illnesses were just psychosomatic. As management consultants and swash-buckling CEOs wielded the knife, the human cost was high. Though, ironically, their actions did not, in the end, protect shareholders when the stock market halved in value during 2000–2003: their wealth disappeared into the ether along with all their employees' lost lifetime.

Increasing numbers of business people, columnists and economists too, now question whether traditional, or neo-classical, economics has caused a rift between the health of society and the strengths of community and the numbers on the balance sheet. For until the real costs of business are calculated, with the wear and tear on employees included on the debit side, people suffer. And, as I seek to show throughout this book, whenever there is a disconnection between God and Money, it is always the individual who suffers. However, over a longer period organisations suffer too. Charles Handy advises that we should think like actors, strutting our brief hour upon the working stage in portfolio career stardom. While this gives a more glamorous edge to present realities, it goes against the grain for most people, who prefer to show the same qualities of loyalty and commitment in their professional lives that they prize and nurture in their private lives. Too bad.

Now it seems that as costs mount, work–life balance issues are rising up the agenda of government and business through-out the industrialised West. But how did we arrive in the UK at such a very bad work–life imbalance? There appears to be more quality of life on mainland Europe, more lifestyle goodies in the United States. Why do we appear to have the worst of both worlds?

In the last chapter I discussed debt; in the next, I shall look at the politics of land. Both, I suggest, play a fundamental role in the stressed-out working lives of people in the UK. As we have seen, debt places so many of us on a treadmill, servicing debt built up just because we are so busy working. We can't downshift even if we wanted to. What would Samuel Smiles say about our current poor borrowing habits in the UK. 'Every man ought so to contrive to live within his means. This practice is the very essence of honesty. For if a man does not manage to live honestly within his own means, he must necessarily be living dis-honestly upon the means of someone else.'[9] Ouch. Economy for Smiles was the mother of Liberty. We may dismiss such flowery sentiments as irrelevant. Yet debt cuts down freedom for manoeuvre; it dictates work–life imbalance. Debt steals hope.

But what about land? I shall discuss this in the next chapter, but it is worth perhaps pointing out that in the UK, people are servicing mortgages and rent levels predicated on an artificial land supply. Just 7.5 per cent of the land mass. It was a leading businessman, the Quaker George Cadbury, who identified what health and happiness could be delivered by unlocking the land. 'Assuming that nine million households could be rehoused in cottages and gardens numbering ten to an acre, this would require not a million acres out of the 77 million acres in the United Kingdom, but probably not half this number would be found needful . . . The wealthy hold the land, millions of acres of which provide for a mere handful of men, sport such as hunting, shooting and racing . . . Those who have fought our battles and saved the Empire ought, on their return, to find room in their own land and healthy homes to dwell in.'[10]

A recent Joseph Rowntree report underlines this,[11] but, as we know, land distribution has not happened. And so we must live with the following grinding equation: market economy + feudal land patterns + debt = a poverty-stricken work–life balance. Plus, I would also suggest, low productivity. So where does God fit into this equation?

The good news is that some companies are waking up to what this situation is costing in low staff retention, recruitment and absenteeism. *The Sunday Times 100 Best Companies to Work for, 2002* survey[12] revealed some imaginative management practices in the UK private sector to tackle work–life imbalance and retain staff. The winner was the supermarket chain Asda, where older workers are given three months unpaid winter holidays, known as 'Benidorm Breaks', and there is widespread flexitime. Computer giant Microsoft encourages staff to join the 9–5.30 club, and donate 10 pence to the NSPCC each time they go home before 5.30 p.m.

Human rights legislation in the UK has helped shift attitudes as well as a tight labour market and recent expensive high-profile cases of companies being sued for employee stress. New maternity and paternity rights, and the right to ask for family-friendly working practices introduced in April 2003, are also helping to reduce absenteeism, especially among women. Whatever the levers, more enlightened employers are working creatively with work, in job shares, teleworking, homeworking, annualised hours contracts, sabbaticals and hours built around the school day, or school term.

This is timely, for it seems the peasants may at last be starting to revolt. Just as brands are vulnerable to consumer-led revolt, so human capital, when it can, is increasingly voting with its feet – out of the door. Corporate greed among senior management and the shareholder-driven selfish corporate governance has led to a growing stampede for early retirement while the pension going is good, for older people. The young are not going to hang around to repeat their parents' experience. The most recent UK census revealed that 600,000 young men have emigrated since the last census, a vast loss of human capital.

'Young people now want a life–life balance,' one management consultant ruefully observed recently. 'Managers need not so much golden bullets to attract the best talent, but golden buckshot, small, well-thought-out, individually tailored inducements to motivate their best people.' After two hundred years of industrial and technological revolution, are working people in the West deciding to cut themselves some slack?

Perhaps it was 9/11, the world's worst attack at work, which accelerated the cultural shift already under way in the West. Those mobile phone messages to loved ones on that terrible day shocked us into reassessing what work is for. Two weeks afterwards, cleverly capturing the zeitgeist, *The Financial Times* ran some articles titled 'Spirituality At Work',[13] looking at the growing need to find a purpose for work. Profit and money were no longer enough in a prosperous West which has all the goodies it needs. Life is short and precious. Time is wealth. So what is my time worth to you?

Whatever our current take-home pay, we owe it to ourselves to audit how our work balances with the rest of our life. We can't allow work to grind us down into a poverty of spirit, for sustainability will be the watchword for survival, for good health and a happy life in the coming uncertain years. I recall the wise words of a self-employed girlfriend, who, in spite of periodic cashflow challenges, has achieved a great work–life balance: 'If I've got to work till I'm ninety, I'm pacing myself!'

5

$£$£$£$£$£$£$£$£

GOD MADE THE LAND
FOR THE PEOPLE

'I suppose . . . men will be emotional and sentimental. They will shed sad tears when they see [other] men moving down the centre of the stream. They will depvise well meaning schemes to pull those fellows out of the stream, but they will never think of going up the stream to see who threw them in.'

Andrew McLaren MP

'When I help the poor I am called a saint, but when I ask why they are poor, I am called a communist.'

Archbishop Helder Camaro[1]

AUTHOR'S HEALTH WARNING: A dear minister friend once said to me that Jesus wanted me for many things, but a sunbeam was perhaps not among them! This chapter is the story of an extraordinary personal journey in just two and half years, which began in baffled ignorance and ended up as an opportunity to make a contribution to real social change. The following pages are therefore a rollercoaster, and not for those of a weak or nervous disposition.

Warm-up exercise 1: stand up and shout, 'Get off my land!'
Sorry, not loud enough. 'Get off my land!' Bit louder.
Last time. Roar. '***GET OFF MY LAND!***'

Not a sentence most of us will ever say, but it is extraordinary how many people have told me that just yelling it out makes them feel a million dollars.

I have spent years writing about how management training can unlock employees' feeling of 'empowerment', yet so
much of today's so-called workplace empowerment is a
smoke and mirrors illusion, designed to make exhausted, overworked employees feel slightly better about life, so that they
will work harder. This exercise of mine, on the other hand,
cuts to the core of who we are and what we are doing on this
earth.

This chapter has not been an easy one to write, for it is
about a giant scam; without doubt, it is the biggest scam I
have ever written about. Its scale is so huge it took me months
to understand how it has been perpetrated for so long on so
many. It is the biggest, most costly gulf between God and
Money there is. It is one which costs all of us in the UK lots of
our money every day of our lives, robs us from putting aside
adequate money for our old age and conditions our entire
national psychology. When this chapter begins to discomfort
you, which it almost certainly will, please don't stop reading,
just shout, 'Get off my land!'

So, Who Really does own Britain?

August 2001. I am sitting in a tent at the Edinburgh International Book Festival listening to an Irishman who speaks
so quickly that I can barely pick up what he says. His name is
Kevin Cahill, a former researcher for *The Sunday Times* rich
list, that annual Bible of the Haves, where readers somehow
invariably end up feeling sorry for those bottom of the ladder
worth just £50 million. His book, *Who Owns Britain*, is, the
audience is told, groundbreaking.[2] All Edinburgh Book Festival
books are groundbreaking. For three weeks hundreds of
groundbreaking books churn up so much intellectual life and
turf in Edinburgh, it take us all months to recover. But this
one is far more than that. For me, it proves life changing. For
Who Owns Britain is nothing less than an extraordinary
investigation into the hidden facts behind land ownership in
Britain.

Cahill charts the extraordinarily successful official concealment of land ownership in the UK since 1872, when the so-called Second Domesday Book, *The Return of Owners of Land, in England, Scotland, Ireland and Wales*, which itemised exactly who owned what, was quietly buried from the view of academics and historians for over one hundred and thirty years; government librarians even refused to admit it existed. This brilliant obfuscation was engineered by the establishment, from the Crown down, and fostered the laughable PR spin that landowners are merely custodians of the nation's heritage (in a good-natured, rather absent-minded and kindly manner). An Orwellian distortion of the truth, even more effective and devastating to us all financially than the language metamorphosis of debt into credit I discussed in Chapter 3.

Some killer facts: the UK is 60 million acres in size. Fifty-nine million of us live on just 7.5 per cent of the land mass, that is, 4.4 million acres. Between 12 million and 14.5 million acres are roads, industrial land, water, forest and mountains, which leaves 40 million acres – around two-thirds of the land mass – owned by just 189,000 families. This number, roughly the population of Aberdeen or Luton, is composed of aristocrats, landed gentry and baronets, who each year receive around £4 billion in subsidies from taxpayers, even though the Treasury has no exact knowledge of who owns what, nor of the income derived directly from land. In England and Wales, the Land Registry estimates that roughly 18 per cent of land is still to be registered, and aims to complete the Registry through voluntary registration by 2012, although it admits this is likely to be more than 18 per cent of land acreage.[3] Cahill confirms that this could be as much as half the acreage of England and Wales, given that a third of the UK as a whole has not been bought or sold since 1928 and has remained unregistered until now.

The power and influence of these hitherto unaccountable, unregistered landowners stretch into every area of political, public and business life; many no doubt do a first-class job. However, in an age of transparency, democracy and 'empowerment', the fact remains that, as a result of land grabs by William the Conqueror, Oliver Cromwell and the deeply clever Plantagenets, 99.9 per cent of the UK population is currently squeezed and squashed on to 7.5 per cent of the land mass. We just do not know that we are. To quote Cahill, 'This is perhaps the most astonishing case of calculated civic deceit ever performed on a whole country.'[4]

You don't need a degree in economics to work out the consequences of supply and demand with such an artificial land shortage. The 7.5 per cent figure instantly explains the UK property bubble, and our own back-breaking £691 billion + mortgaged servitude. It explains why ex-pats can buy beautiful houses abroad for a fraction of the cost of a house in the UK. But spiritually, too, it also explains our national *idée fixe*, the sick fiction of the 'housing ladder', which breeds constant discontent and distance from God. This ladder allows selfish, destructive people to be given the benefit of the doubt for years because of the bricks and mortar they own. While our personal identity is wholly wrapped up in what our small house is worth, its value greater than the sum of all our love, creativity, professional success, good work and faith.

Finally, it explains the growth of the financial services industry, not least in Festival Edinburgh, where the expertise required to create the debt vehicles to service property transactions designed for a skewed land supply has developed over centuries. The very meaning of mortgage (a bond until death) and mortgagee (bondsman until death) are feudal terms of servitude. And with a growing population that is showing ever more Garboesque signs of wanting to live alone, this artificial market has been driven up to current levels of six times earnings.

I sat there processing. My main wonderment was why no one had ever questioned this reality before. Assertive middle classes can fight plans for airports or centres for asylum seekers in their backyard, but when their children have to move away to bring up their families in smaller, highly mortgaged accommodation, they never question the justice of the land-ownership patterns in their own local area. Perhaps the penny just failed to drop that the cornerstone of our post-war prosperity was an illusion, that the middle classes would initially be squeezed and then screwed into the ground.

Now I am an unlikely revolutionary. An ex-trustee of the Chiswick House Friends in London, I have happily stomped round more National Trust properties than you can shake a stick at, and enjoyed fine hospitality and friendships within the 'county set'. I also defend to the death the idea that the law of property is sacrosanct. As I sat there in that Festival tent, suddenly I felt I was living in an upturned world. I had been brought up to believe the Green Belt was a wonderful idea, yet I could now also see that it was an artificial ring-fence around cities to keep rural land off-limits to ordinary people to live on, and keep house prices high, so everyone had a stake in the status quo.

The apparent democracy of the council house sales, which undoubtedly delivered enormous happiness and freedom at the time to many people, was also a marvellous wheeze by the landowners' party. The beneficial side effect was to bring more people into having a stake in high house prices, based on an artificially tight supply. State-delivered disinformation created the Establishment-endorsed myth that we live on a tiny over-crowded island bursting at the seams, and concreting over it should be resisted at all costs. This has been swallowed by politicians of all parties who, not knowing the true statistics, because they do not know the 1872 book ever existed, work with statistics based on this false reality.

I remember reading F. Scott Fitzgerald's story, 'The Diamond as Big as the Ritz', where the family who own a diamond mountain bribe mapmakers to conceal their high-carat stash. Ours is not just a mountain, but a whole country, the shape of which has been distorted by our trusted ruling elite. Millions fought and died in two world wars defending this green and pleasant land; a land fit for heroes as long as, when they returned, they did not expect to take up too much room.

This was disturbing. I picked up my press copy and, ruffling through, looked for the data on counties I knew best. Ayrshire: 33 per cent of the land owned by 196 people; Oxfordshire: 43 per cent of the land owned by 304 people; Hertfordshire, my own home county: 34 per cent owned by 153 people and, finally, where I was then living, East Lothian. 'Easy Living' was the council motto on its brochures and plastic bags. It certainly was for the 100 people owning 56 per cent of the land. Half the population own nothing, and I knew from a friend that if you wanted to grow food for your family on an allotment, the Council waiting list was twenty-three years.

I had a column to write for a Scottish business readership. Where could I start? If it is an economic given that access to land unlocks entrepreneurship, how could Scotland's own land-ownership pattern – the worst concentration of land in private hands in the world with 1,252 families owning 66 per cent of the land – have nothing to do with the lack of dynamic entrepreneurs in Scotland?[5] This topic has come up without fail at every single chamber of commerce meeting I have ever attended. Could landlessness explain why young Scottish males are committing suicide at a rate of 500 a year, twice as high as England and Wales, with a further 10,000 more young men deliberately harming themselves?[6] I could definitely feel a column in the making.

The old Leviticus line came into my head: 'The land shall not be sold in perpetuity, for the land is mine; with me you are but aliens and tenants' (Leviticus 25:23). This was the Old Covenant with Moses and God, the property deal for a Promised Land . . . Could Scotland's business environment be the result of land grabs and landlessness? The Highland Clearances brought economic benefits for landowners, but had clearly damaged the people psychologically and spiritually. Yet the influx of brawny Highlanders into the Clyde Valley and northern English cities delivered much of the labour pool for the Industrial Revolution. I now had my column for this week. Always a relief.

Yet this scam – really it is hard to find any other word for it – is perpetuated on us all, and by the very people who could ask the questions on our behalf: lawyers, chartered surveyors, property developers and town planners. Good friends in all these professions clearly thought I was tip-toeing on to the most dangerous territory and warned me against thinking about it. They refused even to read the book. It was hard not to imagine that, in a previous age, they would have burned the whole print run in a bonfire and denounced Kevin Cahill to the Inquisition. What was going on?

The following week I interviewed the Chairman of a leading housebuilding company, who had a more open mind, but who told me it was the planning restrictions and absence of land for housing that was the main problem. Even he, a successful businessman, had bought the line. But there is no shortage of land, just a monopoly of land values that allows land to come on to the market at the right point in the economic cycle to suit landowners, many of whom, from dukes downwards, have registered the land title offshore. I have friends, far braver than I, who have been up in hot-air balloons all over the UK. They come back with tales of vast empty spaces, of an almost empty country. It was as if I had run up against the hide of a sacred cow, a false idol to whom no one would say moo.

This book is about God and Money, but Land is the ultimate reality behind Money. It is where real power and influence lies. That is why, as soon as people make money, they buy land and keep others off it. It is why Madonna, the Material Girl, initially battled to keep ramblers off the footpaths near her country seat. It is why the Jews, the Chosen People, were given land, not bags of gold. Land equalled freedom from slavery in the Old Testament and it is no different now. Land, unlike money, is permanent, owned in perpetuity for our children.

Try the exercise again. Get off my land! Boy, don't these words make us feel rich and connected to the land? 'You can't imagine, Antonia,' a very jolly landowner once told me, 'what a wonderful feeling it is, that as far as the eye can see is *your* land.'

I spent the winter marinating all this like a good cook. And like the rest of the population, whose descendants were cleared off the land in previous generations, I haunted garden centres, dug my allotment, devoured seed catalogues and watched Alan Titchmarsh and *Monarch of the Glen* on TV. I started reading about the Diggers, the extraordinarily brave, devout Christian men and women in the seventeenth century who, ahead of their time, challenged the private ownership and enclosure land and criticised the established church for propping up the class system.[7] They fought the state-backed land grabbers in unlikely places: in Dunstable, now best known for its proximity to Whipsnade Zoo; and St George's Hill, Cobham, in Surrey, now home to rich entertainers and golfers.

I realised that the history I had been taught at school, and what is now popular history on TV, is always explained from a top–down perspective. We see Britain through the eyes of Elizabeth I, or Henry V – Glenda Jackson meets Larry Olivier – and we identify with them because, let's face it, they are more glamorous than our ancestors, whose lives were brutish and short. The powerful always have the best storylines and history rarely records other people's best one-liners. None of us likes to think we are descended from losers, or that we are losers now, but the current situation makes a laughing stock of us all.

This scam was not just attempted in the UK. According to leading UK land economists Fred Harrison and Mason Gaffney,[8] the American Founding Fathers, who were intoxicated by the Rights of Man, based the US Constitution on John Locke's *Treatise on Government*, which claimed that 'every man has the right to life, liberty and estate'. Estate being the word, at the time, for land. As Harrison describes, this gave the Founding Fathers a problem, for they were large landowners who didn't want to lose control of the large tracts of land they had laid claim to. How awkward, if everyone thought they had a right to land. And so the Declaration of Independence was judiciously altered, to the present wording, which still stirs the richest nation on earth.

'We hold these truths to be self evident, that all men are created equal, that they are endowed by their Creator with certain unalienable Rights, that among these are Life, Liberty and the Pursuit of Happiness.'

The pursuit of happiness instead of land. Brilliant. Once again, language has been used to change ideas and foster a useful financial disconnection, which retains power in the hands of the few.

What a Golden Jubilee really Means

In the town where I used to live, the local laird sold a field. Everyone was heartbroken; it was a landscape of timeless beauty, a precious green lung and a short-cut from the school into the town with breathtaking views of the sea. The town's primary and secondary schools were among the best in Scotland. Families moved out of Edinburgh or up from London to send their children there. And you would see crowds of children flocking through the grass after school.

The land was sold for housing. Not affordable housing for young people, who wanted to stay in this pretty town, but, as is so often the case throughout the UK, for five-bedroom executive housing for big six-figure prices. The decision seemed a *fait accompli*, with scant local democracy; the Council took its money, the developer started building and the laird was able to send his grandchildren to public school down south. The houses, when they came to market, were smart enough to inspire executives in the financial services industry to queue overnight in their executive cars, with their chequebooks in their pockets. It was a phenomenon which was the talk of the town.

It took a while for the penny to drop. That it was local people who had paid the price. We had not only lost a precious asset we thought belonged to the town in the purest sense – the laird having always been considered the kindliest custodian of the town's heritage – but the numbers at the local school exploded to more than thirty-five in a class. And the Council,

the laird and the developer cleaned up, while the new homeowners could look forward to twenty-five years of servitude,
paying mortgages on houses built for a tiny fraction of what
they had paid, and occupying land made valuable not by any
efforts of our avuncular laird, but by the energy and economic
activity of the rest of us. The public services in the community
now faced meltdown. Carefully mentioning no names, I wrote
it up in my column and while many whispered their support,
I was duly cut by the laird's wife.

Two Jubilee pictures:

1. A sunny day in June 2002. It is the Queen's Golden
   Jubilee. A hot sunny June day, thousands are packed
   into The Mall in London. TV commentators tie themselves
   up in hyperbole, as the nation celebrates the Best of
   British. I've always had a soft spot for the Queen. That
   day she looked really happy, but I wondered whether
   she or the crowds knew what the term Golden Jubilee
   originally meant?

2. A young preacher, good looking and charismatic, is
   invited back to his home town to preach. All the townsfolk
   turn out to hear him, having heard on the grapevine he
   has come on rather well and it is human nature to take
   credit for any scrap of reflected glory. The town is a
   thriving community, situated at a crossroads of several
   key routes with a hill behind, which the children in the
   town like to climb, to look out over the countryside for
   miles.

The young man reads a passage from the Old Testament, 'The
Spirit of the Lord is upon me, because he has anointed me to
bring good news to the poor. He has sent me . . . to let the
oppressed go free, to proclaim the year of the Lord's favour'
(Luke 4:18–19). Then Jesus closes the book.

Bombshell. As Sir Kenneth Jupp points out, this was
nothing less than a direct attack on the local landowners.[9]
And by a carpenter's son, too! Jesus only has to add one or

two nice remarks about the Gentiles, being as open to God's mercy as the Jews, for these bigwigs to lose their temper and drag the scallywag up to the top of the hill to throw him off. Jesus' ministry is in danger of being ended before it has begun.

He leaves without honour in his home town, because he has rocked the property boat. If everyone started bringing good news to the poor and preaching land redistribution, where would we be? Can't you just hear the locals afterwards? For the year of the Lord's favour was the Jubilee, which in ancient times redistributed the Promised Land among the twelve tribes of Israel every fifty years. Detailed in Leviticus 25, this was a reckoning, when debts within families were cancelled and land restored, in order to cut out the danger of any landowner monopoly. For, as any third-world aid workers will tell you, landlessness = slavery. The practice of Jubilee land restructuring had gone out of favour centuries before Jesus' time. But that reading was a wake-up call to Nazareth's property owners. His ministry would bring the good news to the Have-nots, not the Haves. A key part of his mission statement was that the oppressed shall inherit the land.

And here we encounter another brilliant example of how official language is changed to screen out inconvenient ideas. In English, we are taught that the meek shall inherit the earth, indoctrinating generations of landless peasants to believe that they would get to Heaven only if they kept their heads down.

Human nature, when it comes to land and money, never changes. I am therefore certain that this incident in Luke happened, having myself experienced the over-emotional and hysterical denunciation of so many Scottish aristocrats to Scotland's mild-as-milk land-reform legislation, as a Mugabe-style land grab (as the tabloids maintained). Ironic, given their ancestors' propensities.

Yet, in the UK throughout 2002, Jubilee Year, the real meaning of the Golden Jubilee was not apparently celebrated by the churches. Why? Follow the money. Some denominations own land and shares, and have needed all the land income they could get, after the stock-market falls, to pay clergy pensions. Yet, what an opportunity missed by the churches to connect with the rest of the population, 'the oppressed' in Jesus' words, who struggle daily to keep a roof over their heads in a system designed to disconnect God and Money.

Too often the churches seem more preoccupied with charity that reinforces the status quo, rather than genuine social justice. Of course, the country would grind to a halt without the time, energy and money given locally in voluntary work by us citizens. Yet we should ask the big-picture financial question, as one of E. M. Forster's characters says in his novel *Howards End*, 'what is the good of driblets? . . . these puny gifts of shillings and blankets'.[10] Charity treats symptoms and does as much good to the giver as the recipient – we can see this post-Empire with the amount of useful occupation it has provided for members of the Royal Family – but it is not the same as giving up genuine assets, which would allow the poor to stand on their own feet, and so regain their self-respect.

Demanding genuine social justice through redistribution of assets would transfer power, and so it would take a brave minister to ask a congregation for shares in companies to be assigned, or unwanted land or untended garden to be given to people on Income Support in the parish, or to ask the local laird to tithe land to the community. Or to call on the Heir to the Throne to desist from constantly buying up land in the ancient Duchy of Cornwall whenever it comes on the market, to add to his £300 million a year income. This vignette in Luke gives some idea about what a blinder Jesus played that day in Nazareth. But this was why the thousands gathered to hear him, and equally why churches today of all denominations face an uphill battle for relevance and long-term viability much past 2050.

Theologians and historians will point to growing secularisation, lack of deference, women's liberation, materialism and humanist values to explain the churches' decline. However, I suspect the real reason is that the churches are judged instinctively by ordinary people as accessory to the fact of an unjust status quo, not challenging the real causes of growing poverty and debt. Just follow the money. Land is power, and giving both up goes against the grain of our human nature, even if the Son of God himself pointed out how rich it could make us. Nevertheless, we should remember that in E. M. Forster's book, it is Helen Schlegel's illegitimate son by the poor, unemployed Leonard Bast, and not the grasping, property-fixated Wilcoxes, who inherits Howards End.

The people at the very end of our distorted land-ownership pattern are the homeless. They're always good for a Christmas donation, but at other times of the year highly mortgaged, stressed-out people are easily wound up by newspapers into feeling that homeless people should be hosed off the streets, for the bad impression they give to visitors, or their potential bad effect on house prices. Yet there is a direct connection between house prices and mortgage debts predicated on the restricted land supply and ending up on the streets, as we saw with the story of Jimmy mentioned earlier. And it does not stop there. I learned of one terrifying symptom of their vulnerability from speaking to workers in homeless shelters for young people. Their anecdotes from long experience would indicate that many of the homeless teenagers they encounter have been sexually abused. How odd that nothing is done to bring the culprits to justice, when there are cases from the 1960s and 1970s regularly in the news. Through which gap in our thinking and action does this social injustice slip through? With little hope long term of either justice or a secure roof over their heads, these 'bruised' people really are the bottom line of the UK.

On the Queen's Jubilee weekend, a lucky few were allowed into the Palace Gardens – 'my daughter's garden' as the shrewd late Queen Mother put it – for a pop concert, with a multi-million PR spend attached. The churches and the media celebrated the life and work of a good woman. But the Queen is also one of the country's biggest landowners, and she enjoys huge tax breaks. The convenient smokescreen that Crown lands are considered not to be personal holdings is effectively cleared when we learn from *Who Owns Britain* that, under the Human Rights Act 1998, she would have to be compensated if these lands were ever removed from her by the government.

While the economy is buoyant, there is no popular will to question this issue – it took the recession in the early 1990s to bring about royal income tax. Indeed, until the next property crash, we are all in the loop, servicing the debt on our own pocket handkerchief of land under our houses, which we hope will rise in value. Furthermore, this mortgage debt might mean that our own children will not be able to afford children or, if they do, they may have to bring them up elsewhere, impoverishing all our lives. We are kept in check and are ignorant of who keeps the title of what land around us, registered in offshore property companies, even as our tax burden mounts.

Into the Light After Ninety Years: The Case for Land Value Taxation

What makes life increasingly impossible in the UK is that we are being slowly ground into dust between two millstones. First, the enduring post-feudal land ownership patterns, supported by the state, and, second, the full-blooded American-style market economy embraced in the last twenty years, powered by the Protestant work ethic.

The combination, as we have seen, seems to be driving the UK, particularly in the south-east of England, to the point of nervous breakdown; we are an 'oppressed' population, suffering stress, debt, fractured family and community life, long-neglected public services and our infrastructure falling apart. We now have a National Health Service where catching an infection in hospital is a one in ten possibility and our children have, for the first time in generations, lower horizons than their parents: *Heat* magazine in 2002 showed 80 per cent of their readers surveyed wanted to emigrate.

So why should we in the UK spend all the hours God sends working to service mortgage debt and an overall 41+ per cent tax burden, just to enable the vested, landed interests to stay effortlessly rich? Surely, it can't be right that those who work the hardest, often commuting on appalling infrastructure, are only as rich, or as broke, as the spin on our artificial housing cycle allows?

On the other hand, what is the answer? Do we call for land redistribution, like Jesus did, and risk being thrown off the white cliffs of Dover? Of course not. Then surely we could find some gentler fiscal form of Christian economics that would, over time, encourage greater equity of land ownership, while unlocking it as a benefit for all of us now?

To quote the playwright Sir Arthur Wing Pinero, that very establishment Victorian, 'the future's just the past entered in through another gate'. I was slowly processing all the facts in Kevin Cahill's book, only too aware of how little I knew, when I became reacquainted with a dimly remembered big political idea that I had learned a bit about at school; an idea which for ninety years has dared not speak its name: land value taxation. No, not the most exciting name in the world. But its effect, I have come to believe, could prove to be nothing less than a New Covenant in the twenty-first century between God, human-kind and land, in which money is created for the public good.

Land value taxation, or LVT, means taxing annually the rental value of land rather than depreciating bricks and mortar of our homes and offices, rather than our labour, our jobs, or the goods and services we buy. It is a gentle, socially cohesive means of reconnecting us to the land. LVT fills the gap between God and Money with community wealth, recognising that it is the effort of community as a whole and not the landowner, which gives land its value. For land-owners, in Stuart Mill's famous quote, 'grow richer, as it were, in their sleep, without working, risking or economis-ing'. So, for example, an acre of Caithness hillside would attract little or no tax, but an acre of expensive Mayfair certainly would. LVT is not so much a conventional tax as a charge for the space we use; it is similar to the charge on a parking meter for the space to park our car, paying more to park in the centre of town than in the periphery, where there are fewer facilities.

Abroad, it has proved rather popular – introduced at local, federal or national level in countries as diverse as South Korea, Denmark, Ukraine, Estonia, Hong Kong, Finland, Canada and the United States of America. It effectively cuts out speculator-driven property booms, sorts out empty properties and brown-field sites, which have been kept unoccupied for use as collateral, or to sell at the right point in the housing cycle; while delivering a huge fiscal pot with which to buy improved infrastructure and public services. It is the one tax that, when replacing existing taxes, delivers both social justice and a stimulated economy, by putting a high price on the community, rather than the individual, and in the process reconnects us to the land.

And yet it has been off the mainstream political agenda in the UK for nearly a century. Why? Why have the Churches not taken it up in Jesus' name? In the context of what we now know about land-ownership patterns and the culture of official secrecy, this is unsurprising. For here is a tax, working well in other countries, that would deliver big benefits for the many, rather than the few. Here the few, the landed interests, are naturally happy with a fiscal status quo, with a few enlightened exceptions. To quote Winston Churchill, once a passionate advocate of LVT, landowners enjoy 'the mother of all other forms of monopoly'.

But first let us go back to basics: why do we pay taxes in the way we do? Because we are told that the only way taxes can be collected is by taxing labour, savings, goods, services and jobs. It is the only way because, as we shall see, conventional economic thinking dictates that this is so. We lack the tools of language to consider alternatives and, in the meantime, we grumble and pay up while our politicians are advised by economists conventionally trained to keep land off the balance sheet as a taxable asset. Their great advantage is that, for most of us, tax is a seriously boring subject and our eyes glaze over. But no more. We simply cannot afford this indulgence.

Traditionally, of course, tax has been used to raise money for war. A brilliant means of using ordinary people to help the rich grow richer under the guise of propaganda, for war almost always involves either the defending or winning of land and/ natural resources which are then controlled by the country's elite. Indeed one could argue that war and taxes perfectly represent God and Money fused, for soldiers pray to God for victory and look forward to the control of resources if they win – one thinks of the fierce Christian rhetoric surrounding the 2003 Iraq War – while Money is the fuel to their endeavours. *Nervos belli, pecunium infinitum*, writes Cicero in his 5th Philippic.[11] As Niall Ferguson points out, from expansionist Caesar Augustus demanding everyone register for the census in their home town to Luke 2:1, to squeaky Pitt the Younger, who stuck a 10 per cent levy on income in 1798 to fight France, tax has always been inextricably linked to war.[12] Writing only a few years later in her novel *Persuasion*, the great exponent of financial fiction, Jane Austen, charts the redistributive financial joys of war, in the new riches and social advancement of her brooding hero Captain Wentworth.

The United States used taxes to fund the American Civil War, while tax and two world wars in Britain forged a grim relationship. On the eve of the First World War, income tax was 6 per cent, rising to 30 per cent by the end. In 1939, it was 29 per cent rising to 50 per cent by 1945. Our exhausted impoverished country was still taxing at over 80 per cent by the mid-1960s. Bitter memories. The phrases Sur Tax and Super Tax have passed from our language now, but my father worked himself to a premature death, servicing a combined 97.5 per cent income tax rate: it remains the stuff of my own childhood nightmares.

Land value taxation, however, has enjoyed a rich intellectual history. As a business writer, passionate about building an entrepreneurial economy, I was relieved to see that Adam Smith, the father of free-market economics, was all for it.

'Ground rents are perhaps a species of revenue which best bear to have a peculiar tax imposed upon them.'[13] Smith was a friend of the landowning classes, but he was also a professor of moral philosophy, who could see that social cohesion was good for business.

The greatest exponent however, was Henry George, a printer, turned journalist, turned political economist and magical orator, whose book *Progress and Poverty* (1879) caused an international sensation, and became the best-selling work on popular economics ever published. George set out his ideas in a coherent philosophy which held out real hope of social justice for workers crushed and bruised by the Industrial Revolution. He called for a Single Tax on land rents to replace all other taxes, attracting supporters such as Mark Twain, George Bernard Shaw, Lloyd George, Albert Einstein, Josiah Wedgwood and, that other master financial fiction storyteller, Leopold Tolstoy. Henry George inspired the Georgist movement, one of the two big popular movements in the nineteenth century, the other being Marxism. He lectured all over the world on fiscal land reform and on dragging land back into people's consciousness as an urban resource. 'The tax on land values is the only tax of any importance that does not distribute itself. It falls upon the owners of the land, and there is no way in which they can shift the burden onto anyone else.'[14]

The Georgist movement sparked popular support at a time when the grinding effects of the Industrial Revolution were testing urban populations to the limit. It may be argued that it was a time not unlike our own. Its urban appeal can be shown by the original game of Monopoly, which was devised in 1904 as 'The Landlord's Game', by Georgist Lizzie Magie, who used the Community Chest to show how a land value tax could be raised for the public good, the more land was bought up on the board. Unfortunately, the later version dwelt on speculation and individual land monopoly, with its inevitable winners and mortgaged losers.

Rereading my well-thumbed books on economics, I am amazed by how the land value taxation has been left out, totally ignored, or else waved aside as being discriminatory against landowners. 'Henry George was mad', a very respected business editor told me in 2002. He could not understand why Adam Smith – hardly a flaming leftie – should have thought LVT so effective, nor why eminent economic commentators of our own day, such as Sir Samuel Brittan, had recently written in favour of LVT to pay for infrastructure. Follow the money . . . Yes, the automatic unthinking response seemed a little too pat.

If LVT is mad, then what about the insanity of our current tax system? Ronald Banks, Chairman of the Centre for Land Policy Studies,[15] estimates that the Dead Weight Loss – a business term meaning the loss in foregone enterprise, in lost goods, services and jobs, in time and money spent avoiding current taxes – could total as much as £881 billion in the UK per year, just £30 billion or so more than the personal debt mountain we are currently staggering under. Therefore, hypothetically, if land were taxed, wholly replacing all other taxes, as Henry George originally advocated, the growth of the United Kingdom economy would grow by a staggering 80 per cent per annum. Now such a fiscal revolution is unlikely to happen, but how exciting could such a prospect be for a chancellor who thinks we are doing well if we achieve 2.5 per cent annual growth? Even if these figures are way out, even if land value taxation were introduced in a limited way to replace existing taxes, what growth could be unlocked? No wonder chambers of commerce in the United States are lobbying hard at City level for LVT. Today, as I write this, an e-mail arrives from Virginia informing me that the towns of Roanoke and Fairfax have voted to introduce land value taxation to replace existing property taxes.

So why can't UK politicians consider taxing land instead of people's labour? They have. Back in Henry VIII's time, Cardinal Wolsey unsuccessfully attempted to value English wealth in the 1522 Great Proscription but was defeated, as so many have been since, by aristocratic opposition. Fast forward to the early twentieth century, when Georgist Prime Minister

Lloyd George and Winston Churchill, then President of the Board of Trade, tried to introduce a limited form of LVT in the 1909 People's Budget, following fierce lobbying by 500 local authorities and well-attended public meetings run by Land Societies all over the country. This Budget frightened the life out of the landowners in the House of Lords, who, in spite of such huge popular will, saw it as the thin end of a wedge that would lead to land nationalisation.

Before the defeat of the land tax clauses, however, the Budget did bring the Valuation Office into existence, now used for Council Tax valuations. Scores of Inland Revenue Valuers scoured the country, mapping what has been dubbed the New Domesday. Exact maps were made with details of land, exacting criteria and protocols neatly recorded in neat purple ink. These maps are still legally binding today for footpath and boundary disputes.[16]

As I began to research this huge subject, I realised what an extraordinary slice of British history has been lost, forgotten or wiped away by economists and historians. The Suffragettes, who fought so fiercely for women's right to vote, have now been claimed as their own by the feminist movement. But they started as a huge, popular movement for land value taxation and social justice (which dominated the late nineteenth century and early twentieth century in the USA and Europe); a cause that is as lost in the UK consciousness as that other long and bloody episode in English history, the struggle of ordinary people against the Enclosures Acts, which deprived them of access to land. While the injustice of Highland Clearances has been widely discussed and, in a sense, reclaimed as their own by Scots post-Devolution, in England you will never see popular TV historians dealing with the Diggers or the Levellers. We all enjoy visiting National Trust properties at weekends, but we never reflect on the social injustice against our forebears that they were built on. What is it about land ownership and acquisition which causes such enormous bouts of amnesia? When will Hollywood discover Henry George?

Followers of Henry George have been disappointed in history, because they did not win through in spite of all that huge popular energy. Perhaps it is time Billy Bragg, songwriter and left-wing activist, had a go updating their anthem, 'The Land Song', sung to the tune of 'Marching through Georgia'. Here are a few lines:

Why should we beg work and let the Landlord take the best
Make them pay their taxes on the land, we'll risk the rest
The Land is meant for the people.

Stirring stuff, which must have caused panic among the Tory Party Grandees at the Carlton Club.

There was also at the turn of the twentieth century an extraordinarily rich seam of newspaper cartoons against the land defence leagues set up by the landowners: one in the Manchester *Evening News* caught my eye.[17] Titled 'The Unpopular Turn', it shows a lord in full crown and ermine as an unpopular music-hall turn. As he staggers offstage, he is helped by the Tory leader of the opposition, Mr Balfour.

Noble Artist (re-entering dressing room): No good. They won't listen to the 'Ruined Landowner'.

Mr Balfour: Quick! Jump into this Joan of Arc armour and try them with 'The Saviour Of My Country!'

We think ourselves so sophisticated in this internet age, and yet daily we swallow much more obviously cynical and self-serving turns than this.

It seemed I had reached the frontier with God and Money meeting head to head, with vested interests on one side, and everyone else in the UK – the 99.9 per cent packed onto 7.5 per cent of the land mass – on the other. I had to make sense of it all, in the face of an economic orthodoxy that no one sought to question.

Why is neo-classical, or traditional, economics taken as gospel? And why are its choices presented as inescapable? Leading land economists Fred Harrison and Mason Gaffney describe in detail their research into the extraordinary efforts on both sides of the Atlantic to distort economics language, teaching and practice to bury Georgist ideas.[18] Landed interests were terrified by Henry George, who saw them as an economic drain on the community. He saw the terrible poverty in American and British industrial cities and advocated land value taxation as the means of creating wealth and public prosperity without war or forced land distribution, while breaking what he called 'the recurring paroxysms of economic depression', language reminiscent of UK Chancellor Gordon Brown's well-known allergy to 'boom and bust'.

George's ideas sparked a huge popular movement, for he offered a clear message of social justice and prosperity. Yet powerful vested interests, carving up the resources in the States, bought highly paid economists to change the message and the words which clothed it. These economists subsumed land into capital as an economic category on the balance sheet, and, therefore, it ceased to be a separate entity which could be taxed separately. They then went further, and positioned wages as a form of rent and therefore a potentially good tax base – unlike land. And so the many were taxed to support the few. The idea of land as a resource which could be taxed for the common good was now an Unthought; it was simply not considered. God made the land for the people? Certainly not.

Gradually Georgists were ostracised or lost their jobs as landed money called the shots in the universities. The term 'neo-classical economics' was established to describe the dismal science which conditions the way we live now, to use a Trollopism. This clever marketing language implies the traditional married with modernity, though classical economists like Henry George considered landowners as un-productive parasites. But from a different cultural viewpoint, labour had been despised back in the eighteenth century by the aristocracy, and parasites were rather admired.

The neo-classical economists were helped by the hysteria in the West about communism and its land nationalisation policies, even though this was never part of Henry George's philosophy. The Depression of the 1930s was exacerbated by neo-economic policies which celebrated arbitrage and speculator-driven stock and property bubbles, and advocated taxing labour to make workers work harder. Two world wars brought us into a more secular self-interested age, and we forgot the battles for social justice that our forebears had fought so fiercely. In the UK, the House of Lords further strangled a basic LVT proposal from Ramsay MacDonald's government and, from the 1960s onwards, house price inflation and mass home ownership brought us all into line.

Here is Mason Gaffney's 1994 description of modern economics, the elements of which seem to breed so much voter apathy and dissatisfaction; this could be the subtext of any speech by any twenty-first century politician in office.

> For efficiency we must sacrifice equity, to attract business, we must lower taxes so much as to shut libraries and starve the schools; to prevent inflation we must keep an army of unfortunates unemployed, to make jobs, we must chew up land and pollute the world. The neo-classical approach is a trade off . . . that has a ring of reasonableness to it, but it presumes a zero sum condition. At the level of public policy . . . no one gets nearly what he wants or what he could get. It overlooks the possibility of reconstruction or synthesis. Henry George said . . . we can have it all![19]

So, looking back, the three-day week, hyperinflation, the market-economy booms and busts, the downsizing, the re-possessions, the bankruptcies, all came out of the Pandora's box of neo-classical economics, that is, all about a few people possessing land – and keeping it away from the community.

Here, on the other hand, is a description of how LVT works in practice, written by the Mayor of New Westminster British Columbia in the 1930s, describing the effects of twenty-five years of LVT:

> The single land tax discouraged vacant land speculation and assisted manufacturers. Population and industry have boomed, but land speculation has been buried. This city is believed to have the largest percentage of individually owned unmortgaged

homes of any city on the continent. It now has the largest invested capital per person of any city in the country and this capital is not inflated speculative land value but rather in factories, machinery, stores and goods . . . The tax has made it easy for the businessman and producer to establish themselves . . . has a tendency to reduce unemployment crises. The merchant and manufacturer do not have to carry the dead weight of a large investment of high priced land . . . nor maintain taxes on buildings, machinery and equipment. Here, factories have been able to keep operating when in other cities they have had . . . to close down . . . Real estate developers have played the role of home builders rather than land gamblers.[20]

And this was written in the 1930s when every other city in north America was surviving on soup kitchens.

Could land value taxation deliver a twenty-first-century-style Golden Jubilee for social justice and wealth creation? If Jesus could drag a tax-collector down from a tree, eat with him, and make him cough up Gargantuan rebates, let us at least consider a form of taxation which puts something of the Promised Land into ordinary people's pockets, in the form of good modern public services and restored infrastructure.

Now I know I must play devil's advocate for a moment. How could we separate buildings from land for valuation? Developers manage this beautifully. LVT would not provide an adequate fiscal base yet, where it has been introduced, there is no evidence of national statistical data to support this. What about the little old lady in the big house who has to pay the same LVT as the millionaire next door? As with the Council Tax, she could receive a single person's rebate. It would cost too much to value all the land. If Lloyd George's clerks could do it with pen and ink, why could we not map the land and value it with new technology? And what about housing sprawl concreting the country? Land value taxation does not mean planning controls are lifted. Australian cities with land valuation taxation, such as Brisbane, are attractive for their compactness, because there is every incentive to build on brownfield land first.

I began to write about land value taxation and ask simple questions, trying to piece together how it might be relevant today. I was struck by the reaction of open-minded business people when I discussed it, and how furious others were at the slightest mention. 'You write rubbish!' pronounced one land-owner who nevertheless did admit that Scotland's landowner-ship pattern did have a lot to do with his perception that young people didn't have 'an entrepreneurial bone in their body!' Still, I kept on asking questions. Why is such a tax, which stimu-lates the economies world-wide while delivering social justice, still not up for discussion on our policy-makers' agenda?

I began to grasp the scale of the job that the landowners and their representatives had done and could only admire their strategy. How whole-heartedly we have been duped. New Labour Party apparatchiks, who didn't seem to have heard of Ramsay MacDonald's support for LVT, were bemused. 'LVT? It's as daft as the window tax', said one press officer. Top business people were also as fooled as everyone else. None I interviewed had ever even heard of this political cause, which had dominated so much of the late nineteenth and early twentieth centuries. Some of the biggest business names in the UK looked at me blankly, even though LVT has been the making of some of the world's most entrepreneurial economies. Unbelievably, the Chairman of a leading Scottish financial institution, a devout Christian, even suggested that LVT would be silly in Scotland, because landowning peers use fewer public services than the rest of us!

But to spread a social epidemic, or a new idea, only needs one good connection.

I wrote up the story for the *New Statesman* on 28 April 2002, which, ever mindful of a good headline, titled the piece 'We Should Soak the Landowners'. Not that LVT does soak landowners; experience overseas shows that LVT causes land values to rise, as infrastructure and public services improve. However, the article caught the eye of the Labour leader of Oxford County Council, Cllr Brian Hodgson. He was inspired enough to propose that a taskforce should be set up to examine how a land value tax could be researched and lobbied for. The Conservative landowners on the Council said they felt they had a conflict of interest and walked out, apparently not representing the interests of their constituents after all.

Meanwhile, Liverpool City Council was already lobbying hard for LVT, because so much of its city centre is owned by property offshore companies that will neither sell nor develop; I now understood why, whenever I visit, the centre seems to have so many hoardings and pot-holed car parks.

I gave a speech at a fringe meeting at the Liberal Democrats' conference in Brighton in September 2002. Lloyd George's party had long had LVT in their manifesto, but they seemed to have forgotten it in the turmoil of the market economy during the last twenty years. It will take fifteen years even to begin a reversal, I was told. Now this was a challenge. I couldn't see the UK's infrastructure lasting that long. What else would pay for it?

I chaired a timely conference by the Henry George Foundation UK in November 2002, which discussed how community-created land values could pay for transport and infrastructure. The London Mayor, Ken Livingstone, was already interested in raising revenue from increased property prices for the Cross Rail project across London; hardly LVT, but his transport supremo Bob Kiley, having seen LVT in practice in the States, saw it as a normal practice. Property developer Don Riley[21] estimated that values of land within a 1,000-yard radius of each station on the Jubilee Line Extension in London had gained by £1.3 billion – a levy on which could have more than paid for the total £3.5 billion cost of the new line. We listened spellbound as a valuer from Pennsylvania told us how it is quite possible to separate land value from property value. It does not involve Harry Potter magic nor rocket science. In Edinburgh, a couple of property companies through imaginative and enlightened self-interest proposed paying for infrastructure through capitalising on the rising land values of adjoining land.[22] Neo-classical economists in the audience took notes; it was increasingly obvious that ordinary taxes couldn't deliver. It was exciting seeing people weaning themselves off lifelong accepted wisdom.

I wrote yet more articles, asked more questions, and found that, thanks to the internet, my work started reaching Georgists worldwide.[23] I e-mailed the chief of the Philadelphia chamber of commerce, which has lobbied fiercely and successfully for a land value tax to reinvigorate the city, where there are 35.6 empty buildings per 1,000 of the population. There, the city tax office reckoned that, from April 2003, 80 per cent of homeowners and 54 per cent of small businesses would pay less property tax: good news as small businesses create 80 per cent of all new jobs. I checked out the Sydney City Council website and saw how LVT wholly funded one of the most enviable and exciting city economies in the world. I learned that LVT was introduced into the British colony of Hong Kong in the 1850s when Lord Aberdeen realised that, as the land was merely leased from the Chinese, there could be no monopoly of land values. How infuriating that his administration had not seen fit to unlock such entrepreneurial dynamism in the UK.

Suddenly, connections were happening all over the place. On 28 November 2002 I chaired the first public meeting on land value taxation in Edinburgh for decades, titled 'Time to tax land and not people'. E-mailing networks all over Scotland, suddenly my colleagues and I had managed to put the tax, which had dared not speak its name for ninety years, back into the public arena. That night, standing up on stage talking about LVT seemed to me pure Christian economics, putting community good into the gap between God and Money. There was a positive constructive debate. More newspaper articles followed, and slowly the momentum grew.

On 30 January 2003, the enterprising Scottish Green Party, spurred into action by the meeting, devoted its one annual debate in the Scottish Parliament to land value taxation.[24] The motion was that the Scottish Parliament should consider and investigate land value taxation for the people of Scotland. It was passed unamended, an extraordinary result for a nongovernmental proposal, guaranteeing political and civil servant time. In London, too, there were plans being made for an early day motion at Westminster, and government officials began to find LVT an interesting topic for discussion. On 1 May 2003, seven Green MSPs were elected to the Scottish Parliament with LVT high on their agenda.

This sort of baptism of fire rarely happens in ordinary daily life. However, just occasionally when we have the opportunity to make a chance connection, we have our own mini damascene conversion when we see the light. In this moment it seems God decides we have work to do, in spite of our ignorance and fear of asking simple questions. In just ten months, I went from knowing zero about land value taxation to hearing my words read out in Parliament. Extraordinary, but it was thanks in part to generous experts in the field like Fred Harrison and Ron Banks who took the trouble to explain. Knowledge, like land, is power, and is so often kept away from us, particularly when it is anything to do with money.

Land is, without doubt, the biggest disconnection between God and Money in the world. But it does not mean we can't talk about it and pray. God made the land for the people, so what are we waiting for?

Case Study:
How Land Taxation Works Today – Barbados

Barbados measures just 166 square miles. Its Government levies an annual land tax on the 94,457 parcels of land currently registered on the land tax register. These include land holdings for commercial, residential and agricultural use, as well as public service provision such as roads, schools, parks and so on. The annual tax rate is 1 per cent on unimproved land valued up to $100,000 (£33,000) Barbadian dollars, with 1.5 per cent p.a. payable over this. Land owners also pay 0.4 per cent on improved land up to $500,000 BDS (£167,000) and 0.75 per cent above. The tax is spread fairly across all sectors and all individuals; rebates are given for pensioners, and for villas rented out to tourists, hotels and agricultural land. Rebates totalled $1.2m BDS (£400,000) in 2002.

The key is complete transparency of land ownership, something its ex-colonial master has still to achieve. This has contributed to a rising prosperity which, though vulnerable to tourism downturns, has led to Barbados's being ranked by the UN as one of the top ten developing countries, with life expectancy and literacy levels now at First World levels.

In the UK, Land Value Taxation is considered, predominantly by the Liberal Democrats and the Green Party, as a possible replacement for property based taxes. But there is no reason why, given the political will, imagination and willingness to challenge accepted wisdoms and bureaucratic empires, land value taxation should not come to replace income tax or national insurance which, with the current overheated property market, lie so heavily on us all.

6

$£$£$£$£$£$£$£$£$£

WHY THE MARKETS NEED GOD MORE THAN HE NEEDS THE MARKETS

'The public be damned. I'm working for my stock holders.'

William Vanderbilt

'If you're not at the cutting edge, you're taking up too much space.'

Enron company motto

'People of the same trade seldom meet together for merriment or diversion, but the conversation ends in a conspiracy against the public, or in some contrivance to raise prices.'

Adam Smith, *The Wealth of Nations*

THUMP. Thump. Thump. Dry mouth and heart beating far too loudly, the microphone is surely picking it up. The muscles round my jaw seem to have contracted so tightly; will my mouth open when I want it to? Will any voice emerge?

It is 10 January 2002. I am sitting in an empty studio in BBC Scotland in Queen Street, Edinburgh, waiting for my live slot on Radio 4's *Thought for the Day* during the *Today* programme. The producer's assistant has talked me through the timing. I have promised myself egg and bacon for breakfast somewhere the other side of eight o'clock.

I am introduced. Now in our Edinburgh Studio . . . Antonia Swinson. Who's she? From somewhere, an oddly young-sounding voice is speaking the words in the script, approved the day before by the *Thought for the Day* producer. SMILE, I have written in the margin. SLOW DOWN. SMILE.

'Jesus famously said how hard it was for the rich to enter the Kingdom of Heaven, but it was the disciples' reaction to this which has always interested me. "Then who can be saved?" they asked him, as if only the rich has the had the economic muscle, which could possibly buy salvation . . .

I've managed not to swallow/fluff words/rustle the pages . . . so far.

A microsecond of silence could crush a Mr Atlas with its weight. Paragraph Three. I discuss some brand-new research from the University of Warwick, which attempts to put a tangible price on happiness.[1] Researchers have worked out that though a thousand-pound windfall measurably boosts our well-being and reduces stress, a happy marriage delivers happiness equivalent to £70,000 per annum. Divorce is calculated at a cost of £132,000, while prolonged ill-health costs £500,000.

It seems hours have passed, but I'm just on Paragraph Four. Now it's time to mention the unmentionable – 9/11. Suggest amid the horror it is an opportunity. 'For this was the day the market economy finally showed the cracks in what it could deliver, and we rediscovered that money can't buy what is beyond price, and that what is priceless cannot be sold . . . all the financial muscle of those investment bankers who rushed down the stairs of the Twin Towers could not be traded for the public spirit of those poorly paid fire-fighters who were treading up . . . We have now all been given permission to reassess the other precious assets we may hold and enjoy: public service, community spirit, family, good health, friendship and faith. Even the rich cannot guarantee for themselves good health, fertility nor physical safety' (SLOW DOWN, SLOW DOWN) 'we must realise that we are all more wealthy than we think.' Silence. Back to the studio.

Broadcasting live is not everyone's cup of tea. Knees almost buckling, I stagger out into the foyer, where the caretaker is bringing in the newspapers. A cab arrives to take me home. I can almost taste the bacon.

The idea that 9/11 gave us a chance to reassess our lives was not new. I had written something similar in my newspaper column earlier and, as the script had followed all the BBC's tight guidelines, I felt it was a reasonable, inoffensive argument, yet one designed to make people feel a bit better about the cold winter morning, as they set off to work.

Next day, my brother rang. 'Have you read the *Telegraph*?' There, in the leader column of that day's paper: '*Thought for the Day* makes me want to smash the radio', with my own script dissected in the fiercest critical terms.[2] I received supportive calls from the BBC Religious Affairs department and a good write-up from the senior producer.

What had so offended the *Daily Telegraph*? Why was the suggestion that it was now time to start reassessing the market economy in the terms of non-financial criteria so offensive? I had not then appreciated that the need to keep the people in the dark was built into neo-classical economics. I had not been criticising investment bankers (rather charismatic individuals on the whole), just the limitations of the system they work in and the inevitable crunching down of the human spirit, when it has to operate in an economic system where only money counts.

Luckily that week, supporting my contention, two high-profile and successful senior managers in Legal & General and the Britannic Group announced that they were giving up their top jobs to spend more time with their families – to the general astonishment of the investment community. Against a backdrop of increasing interest in ethical investment and corporate social responsibility, what on earth could be so revolutionary and offensive in my short slot? Did the establishment dislike one obvious after-effect of 9/11, which was that we, the huddling masses who are not supposed to question the going-for-the-burn work ethic that keeps asset prices so conveniently high, were yearning to be free?

Of course, with hindsight, we now see perhaps a little more clearly that 9/11 was not only a wake-up call to the West, in forcing a reappraisal of how it was perceived and accelerating the growing interest in spirituality already bubbling under the surface. But there were other financial effects too. The presses printed money and pumped it into the economy, and US and UK shoppers went into overdrive. Furthermore, 9/11 was developing into a brilliant excuse for company failures that were already looming before the twin towers fell and provided a breathing space for corporations, in this atmosphere of patriotic fervour, to keep the suckers in the market as the insiders bailed out. As 2002 unfolded, the subsequent war against terrorism was also a useful diversion for the hawkish US government in steering the nation's gaze towards war and away from the spluttering economy.

It seemed too, during 2002, as if Western capitalism was continuing down the path of one of its periodic crises and starting to buckle under the strain of its economic mores. For this was the year that revealed just how far business had perfected the art of not being accountable to anyone or to any community, not even shareholders. *Plus ça change.* As J. K. Galbraith points out in his book *The Great Crash of 1929*, financial insanity can be a source of pure enjoyment when it is someone's else money being lost and not yours.[3]

Other people's money means the savings and pension funds of ordinary people. Just five weeks before my *Thought for the Day* slot, Enron, the Houston energy giant, had gone bankrupt – the biggest losses in global history, at around $80 billion (£55 billion) and, throughout 2002, this was followed by other names which will be the stuff of business courses in the future. Exciting times to be a financial columnist, for this was swiftly followed by Mississippi-based WorldCom, America's second biggest long-distance telephone operator, which went down for $41 billion. Arthur Andersen, auditor to both companies, soon bit the dust. A company reputation, built on years of people not seeing their families grow up, had disappeared, almost overnight.

Then, later in 2002, came the third biggest bankruptcy: that of US insurer Conseco, which collapsed owing $51 billion, followed by the *bombe surprise* of supercook Martha Stewart under investigation for insider dealing. All these US cases could be neatly summed up as being about breaches of integrity, in a culture where the average life of a CEO is three and a half years, with no division between Chairman and CEO as in the UK. Enron had grown so huge, the banks had stopped requiring security and future profits were borrowed against, with earning per share enhanced by financial vehicles such as split capital investment trusts. The Securities and Exchange Commission approved and whistle blowers were not exactly fêted. Was it possible for the professionals on Wall Street to gauge the cold fury of Main Street America, or to imagine how costly the disconnection could be long term?

Next, it was Ireland's turn, when Allied Irish Bank discovered that one of their currency traders, John Rusnak, had run up losses of almost £500 million via complex derivative-backed bets against the Japanese yen, a process designed to transfer risk, which, in fact, produces volatile speculation. I was not surprised to find that Rusnak was a born-again Baptist Sunday schoolteacher. As Keith Tondeur says, Christians have no monopoly on financial prudence. Nor honesty, if the bucks can make a difference to their material standing in their community. Sentenced to seven and a half years in Federal Prison, Rusnak accepted full responsibility without bitterness, saying that he hoped this would lead to his redemption in later life. Redemption. He admitted that his manipulation of the Bank's computer system had allowed him to earn performance bonuses of $650,000+, when the reality was millions of dollars in losses. As 20 per cent of the workforce were subsequently laid off after the bank was sold off, what price redemption?

In the UK, investors and corporations have vacillated between fear and complacency. Every time a government minister or some well-oiled City guru was wheeled out to say it could not possibly happen in the UK with its nice, neat compliance culture, where everyone works in a golden glow of commonsense guidelines and best practice, there were howls of hollow laughter.

It was as if Nick Leeson, who brought down Barings Bank, gambling £869 million, had been a pantomime figure of the collective imagination, and those poor bondholders who were ruined by his trades, a mirage. Back then, in the summer of 1995, Bank of England Governor Eddie George had been widely reported as thinking it unlikely that such a catastrophe would reoccur. However, a similar scam – this time for 'just' $1.1 million – was uncovered the following month in New York, where a trader, from the Japanese securities house Daiwa, was found, like Leeson, to be running both front and back offices.

So where could we put our money with confidence? Then defence giant BAE, Cable & Wireless and MyTravel enraged investors with bad news, which many felt could and should have been announced sooner; changes in more rigorous accounting procedures saw black holes opening up in market stalwarts such as Amey Plc. The Enron effect was by now felt by Abbey National, which was forced to write off nearly £100 million in bad loans. Standard & Poor's made dire predictions on the health of the UK banking system if there were a collapse in UK property values, though these seemed to be the only booming bit of the economy.

Next was the turn of the investment community, as analysts were put against the wall. Thousands of individual and institutional investors threatened to sue, after conflicts of interest revealed that analysts were hyping companies, in order to win more corporate finance business for the banks. So an investment described as 'a piece of crap' in one e-mail soon became a 'Buy' on the market. Everywhere, investors realised they had bought a basket of dud shares from names as platinum-plated as Merrill Lynch, Morgan Stanley, First Boston and CitiGroup. Ten banks eventually stumped up $1.4

billion to settle a case that was being brought against them by New York's District Attorney, Eliot Spitzer. But the price in lost trust was high and lasting. Politicians scrambled to talk serious soundbites about probity and standards but, as they had been bought and sold by corporations for years, no one bought the message and the markets continued to slide. Every time the market went up, people sold off their shares in order to get their money out while the going was good. The UK was no island in this financial meltdown, with British pensioners in particular counting the cost of losses which ate into their basic living standards. This unfairness rewarded those in debt paying low interest rates.

But why did the professionals not see both the scandals and the market falls coming? There seemed to be an expensive and all-pervading complacency. 'No one could have foreseen falls from 6900 to 4000,' a very grand name in the City drawled to me in autumn 2002. Why not? I wanted to retort. But I realised I was mistaking his superb insouciance for complacency, when in fact he was merely adhering with great style to the official economic orthodoxy.

It was J. K. Galbraith who coined the term for this orthodoxy: preventive incantation. This means talking up the market at all costs. Preventive incantation means that until the herd switch to talking down the market, usually when they have been found out, to the point that no one is buying anyway, then we never, ever talk down the market, whatever the reality, the fears, the truth, our own doubts or scruples, or the obvious consequences to friends, family and neighbours. *Cantare* in Italian means to sing, *incantare* to enchant. And the City is a noisy, musical, spellbinding bedlam full of enchantment.

J. K. Galbraith observes that whenever people are persuaded of their own wizardry or that of the professionals managing their money, they are soon parted from their money.[4] And indeed the preventive incantation which continued in four-part harmony throughout the autumn months of 1929 and beyond seems very familiar, as leading Wall Street figures back then took care to be seen to meet, to create the appearance of organised market support, which kept investors buying, while they organised their own exit strategies.

I have seen the preventive incantation spell woven on many occasions, social and professional. In the hands of good practitioners, it is certainly very impressive. For it keeps the professionals' jobs, bonuses and pay cheques coming in, and those glass stumps of office blocks that they work in well filled and heated, however costly to the individual saver when the bubble eventually bursts.

If the market is plunging in panic, then preventive incantation is quickly 'magicked' on to TV screens, calling the panic just a prudent 'correction', a temporary pause for breath, before the markets carry on rising to the sunlit uplands, where we shall all be rich. Stay in the market or you'll lose out. There is never a good time to sell the market. Stay in. If we question this orthodoxy, then we are looked upon as heretics; we are gently reminded that history shows that it is always better to stay in the market, which inexorably rises over time. Pessimists are losers. The professionals will not say that future performance does not reflect past performance, that is left to the small print when we first buy. Nor will they admit that, of course, we could always buy again when the market falls if it suits our circumstances better. But they are not interested in us.

So a bit of free disinterested advice here. Follow the money. Let's ask ourselves whom it does not suit if we disinvest. Whenever we are sold a line, given a bit of preventive incantation, asked to buy into a company or even an idea, whether for profit or not, follow the money. Staying in the market as investors means we continue to pay the professionals' fees. If the market falls, and our savings plummet, then we have to be grown up about it. Just don't sell, they tell us. The market is going to rise. It is a historical inevitability. We'll miss the boat, never be able to buy in again. Official.

Preventive incantation brilliantly overrides natural caution, moral scruples of right and wrong, and goes with the flow of natural human greed and our fear of missing out. Estate agents and mortgage lenders are other experts on preventive incantation, helping property bubbles to last until the very last desperate strung-out, over-geared buyer is lured into buying, long after it makes sense to that person or anyone else. But we're talking percentage fees at stake here, too. The fact that speculation damages the fabric of communities is not important. Exploitation of resources is at the heart of market economics. That is the secret of its effectiveness, but also its huge implicit weakness as the moment comes when the bill is presented, when the sums do not add up and nobody has the confidence to buy in.

In City terms, preventive incantation also keeps up the powerful mystique that surrounds big money, the taboo which says to the average person interested in investing that it is best to leave Capital to the professional witch doctors, who understand the portents. Like all the gaps between God and Money, it is very convenient for the witch doctors .

Of course there are many more TV and radio programmes about personal finance now than in previous years, and investment advice in the press has done sterling work in calling financial institutions to account about endowments mis-selling, imploding split capital investment trusts, investment trusts . . . yes, we have had plenty of meat to chew on. But here, too, there is always a measure of preventive incantation.

We financial journalists are wined and dined regularly by the marketing departments of financial institutions. It is not in our interests to rock the boat too much, though the press can help readers develop a nose for preventive incantation and, once primed, readers can spot it a mile off. Ironically, though other areas of the media can be knee-deep in scandal and bad news, we can always find rays of sunshine in the business and money coverage. Why? Partly because business readers and newspaper proprietors need optimism to keep asset prices buoyant – hence the reason why news of housing downturns always follows months behind reality – and partly because so much vitally needed advertising revenue comes from financial institutions. This tension blunts investigative zeal, most noticeably in the disturbing lack of serious investigation into the UK pension industry. In order to boost profitability, every journalist must deliver copy in volumes once unheard of, and so imperceptibly becomes ever more reliant on the PR departments of the big companies, which have huge resources to give us all the copy-ready information they think we need. It is an unequal battle. So we go with the flow, until bad news is inescapable. Our best hope is to try to give readers as much perspective as we can remember. So which of us dares break the spell and cry out that the emperor has no clothes?

When looking at an investment, I would say use your eyes and nose and follow the money; see it from the professional point of view. Preventive incantation is a given. There are some fine investment specialists and, if ordinary investors choose to buy their brand of magic, good for them. I am also not pessimistic about the markets; there are always opportunities for canny investors who sniff out value and invest money they can afford to lose. Don't leave it up to the professionals, though, because they do not always have investors' best interests at heart, whatever they say. If we're lucky, theirs and ours will coincide, but we can't bank on it.

If we buy an equity-based product (and equities are 'by far the most stable and liquid of assets', I am seriously assured by a nice Independent Financial Adviser on a Friday afternoon after the market has dropped 4 per cent in one week), every time we buy and sell, someone gets some of our money. There is a 4 per cent initial start-up fee, from which the independent financial adviser, who originally sold us the product, gets around 3 per cent, followed by annual management charges of 1.5 per cent. Even the stakeholder pensions charging just 1 per cent per annum, which the industry has considered so cheapskate and have lobbied so fiercely against, would still take one-third of our money over thirty years. Now this is all clearly explained on purchase, and of course we hope that the investment will rise so much that the charges will be trifling. But, then, if the market falls, in spite of being talked up as much as it can, we not only lose a percentage of our money, but there is also the cumulative drain of compound deductions for charges. In addition, there is the loss of interest, however measly, it would have been earning in a 'tax efficient' savings account. Three lost sources of income over three years of falling markets soon add up, as so many of us today can attest. Hardly surprising, therefore, that the preventive incantation chorus can be deafeningly loud.

No wonder, too, the City is worried that so many people are voting with their feet and either spending their money instead of saving, or buying to let properties for their pensions.

Our advisers and brokers will rarely suggest we should disinvest from the market, unless we are heading for bankruptcy, because the bigger the number of guests at the party, the bigger the gains. Indeed, 98 per cent of shares traded on the FTSE are buying and selling existing holdings. Every time shares are churned, someone is making money out of us. Hence the old Woody Allen line back in the mid-1970s, about giving his money to a broker who can invest it till there's nothing left. Hence also why during the longest bull market in history, millions of endowment mortgage holders in the UK will mysteriously not have enough to pay off their mortgages.

I think of the speechless fury of one colleague in our local pub one night, who had just received a letter from his mortgage company announcing a large five-figure shortfall, while a neighbour down the road, working for the same mortgage company, brought in the drinks, announcing he had just been given a £20,000 bonus. It is at the local neighbourhood level that calls for change can come. Markets and institutions ignore the power of such community networks at their peril. It is a small world, and that great tool of the little person, the internet, is making it smaller.

What we ordinary investors must always take into account, before we write a cheque, are the stories this sector tells itself, which have echoes of eighteenth-century aristocratic attitudes, when trade was considered vulgar. For neither independent financial advisers nor product providers – the insurance companies – believe that they actually 'sell' anything. The insurance companies say they just create the products, and don't sell anything. It's the IFAs who sell, they say. But IFAs – who by the way are reportedly being lured by these 'non-selling' financial institutions with commissions as high as 8 per cent on investments in some with-profits funds – will tell you that no, they don't sell either: they *advise*. So that's all right then. Nobody sells, so Nobody is to blame. So, when people think they are buying an investment with a guaranteed return, they actually find they have bought a high-risk equity-based product. Tough. Just stay in the market.

This has an unsustainable amorality which few other trades can equal. How different is this from a pimp who says he does not sell sex, it's the hooker; while the hooker says she does not sell sex either, she only shows the customer the possibilities and takes the money?

As I sit writing this chapter, I can hear the noises over the road as removal men are busily moving the contents out of a neighbour's house and into – to use Wall Street parlance – a 'starter castle'. This neighbour is an important player in one of those ten leading merchant banks that were fined $1.4 billion by New York State Attorney Eliot Spitzer. How's this for preventive incantation? In December 2001 my neighbour's employer forecast – albeit with most analysts – that the FTSE 100 at the end of the following year would stand at 5,900. In fact, it ended at 3,941 after the worst fall in six years. Collective amnesia seems to grip the investment banking community when reminded of its bullish predictions at the end of 2002. Yet this was not just a bit of fairground forecasting in the press to keep the financial writers happy. No, lucrative business was being sold to our pension fund managers on the back of these upbeat assessments. Yet where is the accountability beyond a shrug of the shoulders? Barrow-boy economics apparently rule okay . . . Bananas bad when you got 'em home? Not my problem, mate. *Caveat emptor*, old son.

I'm only human. I can't help nosily looking out of the window. I see luxurious objects being carefully carried by white-gloved removal men down the path. It is an interesting exercise reminding myself not to admire unnecessary things. Yes, these have been bought and paid for by hard work certainly, but work that involves making decisions that carry extraordinarily little accountability for others' losses. Other professionals are held accountable for their decisions every day of their lives yet, in the City, at my neighbour's level, heads rarely roll; the redundancies usually slice through lives lower down the food chain. Senior managers in Mutuals also made massive gambles, lost our shirts, but still picked up bonuses at the end of the year, instead of their redundancy payments. In March 2003, as war against Iraq loomed, came news from the USA that, in spite of the fourth year of bear-market performance, Goldman Sach's chief Henry Paulson picked up $12 million, Morgan Stanley's boss Philip Purcell scored $11 million and Merrill Lynch's Chairman and CEO both picked up $7 million.[5] Happy days.

I can see the smirk on the faces of City professionals reading these lines. However, markets are not divorced from real life. I think of novelist Nina Bawden's comment[6] that it was as if the company had blamed little green men from Mars, rather than management negligence, as the cause of the Potter's Bar rail crash, in which her husband died; and the former Railtrack Chief Executive Gerald Corbett's observation that rail privatisation had been designed to maximise returns to the Treasury, not to optimise safety. He neatly moved on to chair Woolworth's plc not long after the crash, announcing on the BBC Radio 4 *Today* programme, with monumental insensitivity, that this was for him 'a new chapter'. Anthony Trollope could have certainly used this in a book.

Business is on a loser, if it continues to take people and their communities as a fixed resource to be exploited for labour and investment. People have already been badly affected by market speculation and unfair taxes. In the West, ordinary people are adding up the sums as ageing baby boomers, weaned on post-war certainties, now reassess and make account of themselves to a new generation. Reputational risk is no joke, as we shall see in the next chapter: it can infect institutions and brands with lightning speed.

If City professionals are lucky, the growing interest and buy-in by companies and investors into corporate social responsibility and the power of socially responsible investment will force a gradual but radical improvement in standards. It will also affirm the importance of community in sustainable business decision-making, and allow some of the pie for small businesses, which create the vast majority of new jobs.

But, if not, the markets have a problem. For why should the majority continue to subscribe to a system of market economics that operates against our interests? It seems we have now reached the endgame in market economics that are unaccountable to people and divorced from their communities.

At the end of December 2002, the *Independent on Sunday* declared that if 2002 was the year of pain, misery and bloodletting, now was the time for redemption.[7] Redemption. There's a word with a huge Christian meaning to describe unrighteous Mammon. So as we investors weep over our lost paper wealth or smugly count our gains, have market economics suffered enough to be redeemed?

Could salvation lie in recognising that 2 + 2 don't always add up to the same result? Markets are composed of all the best and worst human emotions and enterprise. It is why they are endlessly fascinating, never still, always reacting. Yet the 'dismal science' of modern economics celebrates not the colourful vagaries of human nature, but the cool and collected knowledge of mathematics. Mathematics has beauty, but no love.

If there is one lesson to be drawn from the City's *annus horribilis* of 2002 – with its corporate failures, plunging investment returns and the decline of financial asset values – which might help towards our redemption whether as investors, market makers or business leaders, it is the startling rediscovery that the markets need God more than he needs them. For we have seen that taking God out of the equation has made us all poorer. Not just spiritually. Financially, too.

For without shared moral and spiritual values, there is no yardstick of good behaviour, and trust breaks down. As John Noble, Director of the British Brands Group, points out in the recent New Economics Foundation report: 'Trust lies at the core of the relationship with the consumer. No brand can survive long without it. The aim of any successful brand is to earn a deeper level of trust than its competitors.'[8]

Now, post-Enron, and with policy-makers making not very loud threatening noises, it seems courses on ethics are just starting to poke their nose uncertainly on to the Master of Business Administration (MBA) syllabus. But why not some faith-based ethics courses, too, on MBAs, sponsored by major faiths? Such courses could only benefit, because the churches themselves have sustained such huge investment losses through the markets' moral failings. What better way to show the churches' relevance to business?

Ethics share, with mathematics, the beauty of intelligent thought, but how can ethics possibly compete in strength with shared beliefs, experience and culture laid down over the centuries, on which business best thrives? I am spending my time writing this book, because I believe passionately that spiritual values can increase our wealth. For just look at what we have lost without them!

Isn't it time to rattle a few of today's sleek people, ask some awkward questions? Post-Enron debates, organised by clubbable City types, have invariably made me want to vomit. Crocodile tears, disingenuousness, selective memory and superficial analysis, which knowingly do not begin to address our concerns, have been shameless, and all the more painful, when so many of these people profess to be Christians, or have been speaking in Christian forums. In one such event I attended, the audience was actually asked to sympathise with 'poor' City workers, servicing hundreds of thousands of pounds' worth of lifestyle debt. Anyone would think Christian teaching is only for the 'little people'.

Yet Christianity, like all the major faiths, offers us a solid template on how to live our lives in communities; how to curb our worst excesses through peer pressure, how to live good lives with respect for others, in a way that no legislature could possibly equal. However seldom we might feel moved to visit our church, mosque or synagogue, however cynical we may feel about the damage organised religion has wrought throughout history, nevertheless, it is deeply ingrained ethics of faith which create, if not perfect love, then at least respect for others. This, in turn, creates trust and social cohesion on which business networks thrive. Business needs God. So what else is new?

So here is a crash course in religious education, which should be sent to every Gordon Gekko wannabe who wants to play *Wall Street* speculator games, before he starts his MBA.

Judaism:

Rabbi Hillel (60 BCE–10 CE): 'Do not do to others what you would not want them to do to you.' (Shabbat 31a)

Christianity:

Jesus of Nazareth: 'Whatever you want people to do to you, do also to them.' (Matthew 7:12; Luke 6:31)

Islam:

'None of you is a believer as long as he does not wish his brother what he wishes himself.' (Forty Hadith of an-Nawawi, 13)

Buddhism:

'A state which is not pleasant or enjoyable for me will also not be so for him, and how can I impose on another a state which is not pleasant or enjoyable for me?' (Sam Yutta Nickaya V,353, 35–342.2)

Hinduism:

'One should not behave towards others in a way which is un-pleasant for oneself: that is the essence of morality.' (Mahabharata X111 114,8)[9]

As leading Christian economist Kamran Mofid points out, 'neo classical economics has major shortcomings, it con-

centrates almost totally on self interest, and praises individualism and greed; it has little respect for, or understanding
of, the true human values of community . . . common good,
morality, ethics and justice . . . modern economics has deprived
us of knowing God and of appreciating the important role
religion can play in our everyday economic, political and
cultural lives'.[10]

If the markets need God, does God need them? Hardly. He
loves people, not transactions. So when will those big beasts,
blindly number crunching through the corporate jungle, finally
realise that if they stay on their present limited course, they're
bound for dinosaur history? Can't they see that a market
system that fails to rate its fellow human beings to the point
of extremis, so the world's richest 360 people own as much as
the poorest 2 billion, is heading for extinction? Their spin and
glossy PR don't work any more; we are tired of their magic
tricks.

So who needs dinosaurs? We don't. We don't need to buy
from them. As we shall see in the next chapter, the realisation
that the markets need God could be the best news that good
business has had in years.

7

$£$£$£$£$£$£$£$£

ETHICAL BUSINESS – PUTTING GOD WHERE WE EARN OUR MONEY

WE all have to earn a living, but when someone at a party asks where you work, do you mutter into your drink or proudly announce it? Your response, so management consultants tell me, depends on whether your employer's values are in tune with your own. Put into normal language: no one in business wants to work for a godless set of pirates, however good the pay or high the share price these days, because we are too prone to peer pressure and embarrassment. Also, as consumers and shareholders, we are too wised up.

And so welcome to this chapter on the very grown-up world of corporate social responsibility, a movement which, though full of cynical imperfections and lots of dressed-up pragmatism, is still perhaps the most effective means of bringing God into where we earn our money.

Corporate social responsibility is an overarching term to describe the way that companies are engaging in dialogue with their 'stakeholders' – that is, those affected by their operations, such as staff, customers, suppliers and their host communities – about the environment, human rights, health and welfare, and the community life. This may sound like gobbledegook to anyone not in business, or a fancy way of saying what organisations should be doing anyway. Yet it is, at best, an attempt to manage a spiritual and ethical response to the corporate excesses of the 1990s and the crash of bricks through trendy coffee-house windows thrown by the anti-globalisation protesters in Seattle, Genoa and Washington. Best of all, it is good business stewardship – making money and reducing costs. According to one report, 64 per cent of British adult workers would have an improved opinion of their company if it supported society and community, while another European study showed 87 per cent of European employees feel greater loyalty to socially engaged employers.[1] Whether you take these surveys as gospel or not, notice has been served on business to clean up its act.

In part, this rise of corporate social responsibility is a generational shift, as senior managers of the baby-boomer generation now look back at their careers and want to feel they have made a difference. They don't want their children and grandchildren asking them why they work for that awful unethical company. While younger people too, educated on the internet and brought up by time-strapped working parents, put a high price on how they spend their own working life. Recruitment managers on university 'milk rounds' report increasing numbers asking about and comparing the social responsibility policies of exhibiting companies.

That it has all happened so comparatively quickly is obvious when you consider Milton Friedman's famous remark 'the one and only social responsibility of business is to increase profits' was made only in 1970.[2] How dated and out of touch this seems. Of course, there will always be senior corporate executives who will agree with Friedman, but the difference is that, now, it would be very bad business to admit it too loudly!

Why should fully-informed people in business leave personal values at home, particularly when it is so obvious that business needs a fair, cohesive society? Adam Smith is best known for that free-market bible, *The Wealth of Nations*. Yet, as Professor of Moral Philosophy, he also wrote the much less read *Theory of Moral Sentiments*.[3] In *Moral Sentiments*, he set out his belief that it was our sense of justice that was the strongest brake on naked self-interest, even if this arose as much from wanting other people's approval as wanting to feel good about ourselves.

Smith couples the race for wealth uncompromisingly with the fear of God. The language is old-fashioned, but here lies the sustainability of the market ideal, with those in business acting as good stewards. So what's new? 'To all those who have, more will be given' is the line we often associate with the rich getting richer. But this in fact is Jesus' great pay-off line at the end of his Parable of the Pounds, which is about the good steward who wins promotion because he has been 'trustworthy in a very small thing'. Successful business = good stewardship + good conscience. It's not rocket science. How far from God do we think we have to be to make a profit?

In the United States, always more interested in practical Christianity than more secular Europe, there has been a growing movement to foster spirituality at work – a new twist to the Protestant work ethic. It began in the mid-1990s at the World Bank, where staff formed the Spiritual Unfoldment Society. This, in turn, led to a management project to align corporate and spiritual values. Now this may have arisen from harsh criticism by non-government organisations and charities about the effect on developing countries of World Bank policies, but it was an interesting development driven by staff, not senior managers or consultants.

There have since been executive development programmes at cutting-edge firms such as Ericsson and Mitsubishi involving 'love-based values', and Volkswagen and Ford taught sales staff a 'spirit of service to something greater than one-self'. In the Texas offices of Southwest Airlines, corporate literature speaks of a 'higher purpose', delivering Americans to their loved ones. In the USA, there is now a booming market in corporate chaplains, offering counselling and faith-based programmes in the workplace.[4] Meanwhile, MBA students across the West devour the very books that have spearheaded criticism of corporate excess and unlocked consumer discontent.

In the 1990s, activist writers took on the mantle of the social reformer Charles Dickens in taking the debate on globalisation to a mass audience. Naomi Klein's book *No Logo* exposed desperate sweatshop practices of Nike, Disney and Gap to a world-wide audience, and showed how vulnerable these brands were to global reputational damage. George Monbiot's *Captive State* pulled the debate further into the effects of deregulated global corporations undermining our democracy and damaging our environment. Influential journalist Will Hutton set out to re-educate both politicians and the business community, as outlined in his books *The State We're In* and later *The World We're In*. As an Exocet missile to a single sector, nothing equalled Eric Schlosser's *Fast Food Nation*, which went behind the scenes of America's junk-food industry, and led to a widespread reappraisal of its horror-story treatment of animals and meatpackers, a contemporary echo of American author Upton Sinclair's exposé of the industry in his 1906 novel, *The Jungle*. Coinciding with concerns about obesity and BSE, the book was arguably a factor in McDonald's falling profits and restaurant closures. The companies have since given undertakings to improve matters.

For years, I have both written and run training programmes on corporate social responsibility. I've seen how hard it can sometimes be, trying to do business within an ethical framework, for this is not an easy subject as we operate in a world which still considers this issue so much hot air. I have met and interviewed managers who genuinely seem committed to social responsibility in their own departments, yet feel they have no connection with sad accounts of corporate malpractice from human rights organisations concerning the suppliers of their companies. Some of the most evangelical leader companies of corporate social responsibility can also be prone to pick 'n' mix ethics. For example, Boots in the UK has been heavily criticised by investors for chief executives' pay, while Dixons has been lambasted for taking profits offshore. They can't have it all ways. Hypocrisy inevitably shows up the gap between words and actions, and makes bad public relations.

The good news is that businesses are learning fast about long-term effects of reputational damage. For the irony is that at a time when business has apparently never been so powerful for its control over all aspects of our lives, including UK public services, it is also increasingly only the loyalty of staff and customers that differentiate them from the competition in the fight for market share.

Take this in conjunction with the extraordinary power of the internet to start popular campaigns, and it is clear that the tail is going to be wagging the dog rather more than some older business people and politicians are used to. Surf the internet and there is a wealth of well-written and well-informed and imaginative websites chronicling corporate mal-practice in every sector. A few are listed at the back of this book. In the UK, a leading powerhouse is ethicalconsumer.org, run by the Ethical Consumer Research Association, which publishes *Ethical Consumer* magazine. Over the years, I have witnessed some extraordinary transformations in executives' behaviour when I have informed them that their own companies are featured on the website for less than ethical behaviour. In keeping with Adam Smith's view that human beings will seek social justice in order to be well thought of by others, their reaction involves pleading for time and expressions of a desire to reform, rather than aggressive bluster. Here lies a huge opportunity to make a difference. For into this democratisation of customer and business, there is scope for us to bring God into the picture. As the two case studies below show, it is all about having the imagination to make that connection. Or not.

These developments are part of a historic continuum, for business excess always brings about a reaction as the pendulum swings back, as business realises it cannot take host communities, investors or a mobile workforce for granted. Trust has to be earned. It happened before in the nineteenth century; for then the equivalents of the corporate social responsibility leaders of today were called 'philanthropists', such as Robert Owen and the Cadburys, who pioneered better housing and health provision for their own workers. In fact, this was not philanthropy at all, but businesses making adjustments to the political climate. The Industrial Revolution came relatively quickly after the population had been cleared off the land and crowded into the cities. Living conditions were causing the intellectuals to whip up middle-class opinion, while business and government looked over the Channel and feared revolution. Any philanthropy was therefore enlightened self-interest and a form of insurance.

So now we have large businesses considering themselves at the forefront of social change, tackling inequality, poverty and pollution, through creating wealth and establishing best practice in the work place. Yes, it is easy to be cynical but, as this is the opposite of enthusiasm, we just need to ask ourselves which achieves more?

So how do we measure this best practice? Social reporting, how companies demonstrated the effects of these new policies, was slow to start. Enlightened companies such as Body Shop, Ben & Jerry's ice cream and the Co-operative Bank were first in the field in the 1970s and 1980s, in spite of financiers dismissing social reporting as eccentric. But they were later joined by other companies, such as Rio Tinto, BP Amoco and Shell, where reputational damage and share price falls had led to much corporate soul-searching.

Now social reporting and, its natural follow on, social auditing are reaching a critical mass driven by regulation, and increasingly accepted and exacting standards. All this ties up management time and money, as audits can take months observing companies at work. However, it is viewed as money well spent on improving staff morale, recruitment and retention, and relationships with suppliers and customers. Everybody wins when business takes seriously its responsibility for others.

Good corporate social responsibility could centre on quite small changes in organisational life. Staff issues could include policies on achieving a good work–life balance and equality to training and promotion; community issues could include traffic and pollution, and issues around suppliers, for example, could centre on speed of payments. How many small businesses have gone bust through late payers? But the point is, corporate social responsibility means real policies in action, internalised into company culture, not just empty phrases.

You may know J. B. Priestley's play *An Inspector Calls*, in which the pale Inspector Goole calls one night on a well-to-do manufacturer's family and demonstrates over three acts how each member is partly responsible for the suicide of a young girl. It is perhaps stuck in its period, but let us, for a moment, take the role of Inspector Goole and reconsider the case of Jimmy, the *Big Issue* vendor whom I described earlier. Let's work backwards from his death in a doorway on one bitterly cold night in Glasgow in 1998, back to the clients he was supplying, whose managers believed, like so many successful businesspeople, that paying suppliers as late as possible made good business.

If his clients had paid him on time – actually living up to the easy words they had put in their annual reports – then Jimmy could have paid his own suppliers and saved on the sky-high interest he was then being forced to pay the banks. He could have made pay roll and kept his staff, and paid his suppliers, who then would not have gone for a County Court judgement, which preceded the bailiffs and bankruptcy. His home life would also have been happier and so his marriage would perhaps not have failed and his children might still have a father. If we think about the effect of Jimmy's downward spiral and death on so many people's lives, and what a contribution he could have continued to have made as a parent, husband, citizen, employer, client, supplier and taxpayer, then we can see what a huge act of good stewardship just one small piece of good accountancy practice could mean.

Now Jimmy's downfall was more complex than that, but it does so often take one bad debt to bring the whole pack of cards down. This is what I believe good stewardship should be all about: however small our actions, we can still connect God with money and business. Good stewards have the imagination to see how small changes of behaviour can have wider implications.

As David Grayson and Adrian Hodges detail in their excellent book *Everybody's Business*,[5] good corporate social responsibility is the future and can make business money by delivering bigger market share, a better reputation, investor loyalty and employee retention and morale. And there is a lot of good news out there. Shell, which saw staff morale hit rock bottom after the Brent Spar disaster, has launched the organisation Live Wire in the UK to provide advice and mentors to help young people start their own business. Furthermore, other companies such as B & Q and C & A engaged actively with their supply chain in the third world, avoiding the headlines about sweatshop labour which had dogged other high-street stores as Gap or Disney. In 1999, C & A took out advertisements in *The Financial Times* to say that 100 suppliers had been barred, facing workplace audits. Of these, forty were reinstated after taking action to improve working conditions.

Yet connecting God and wealth creation is a long slog, say the social auditors. Companies can be goody-two-shoes ethical and then suddenly announce dozens of redundancies, but changes can be small, notched up a bit at a time. The biggest weapon remains the bad impression given if a company is not engaged in corporate social responsibility. Yve Newbold, former Chairman of the Ethical Trading Initiative, comments: 'Both executive and non executive directors today cannot consider themselves wholly competent to serve on the boards of public companies if they are wholly ignorant of the issues of social responsibility with their companies.'[6]

Now, of course, like any new value system, corporate social responsibility can be taken over by people for short-term self-interest: it can tip-toe in from the PR departments to make the annual report look better; it can be the means that managers use to squeeze an extra pound of flesh from their subordinates under the guise of 'team building' by schmoozing them about the corporate 'family'; or it can emerge from the human resources departments as a means to get away-days on trendy-sounding courses. But the best, most lasting corporate social responsibility comes through the inspiration of senior managers suddenly making the connection and driving company policies forward.

Corporate social responsibility is a process that needs good people with the strong will to shift perceptions and the context of what is acceptable mainstream corporate behaviour. It needs patiently to be layered down like good compost over long periods, before it starts nourishing every area of organisational life.

Good stewardship, however, can be risky: we might not be able to effect change because of falling sales, or lack of training. And, in so many ethical issues, grey is the new black and white. When is a good steward a whistle blower? How long do we bang our heads against a brick wall before we quit? We can toil away on the side of the angels in our department, only for our boss to subcontract suppliers in a developing country, sexually harass a colleague, or sell off our company to a City institution, for what we know is funny money, then cash in and leave. It is not easy.

Yet to be successful and to keep going, we must believe that every small action brings God into where we make our money, tips the balance, and increases the sum of human happiness – not least our own. The corporate social responsibility revolution has sprung from millions of working people who want change, and we have huge power in our hands as colleagues, managers, customers, suppliers, citizens or just as bolshy voices who won't be quiet.

Below are two case studies from stories I covered in 2001 and 2002 as a journalist. They illustrate so clearly, as in the story of Fairway Forklifts, what a huge opportunity business has to contribute to its host community while making money. Or how mere lip-service to corporate social responsibility can become unstuck when a multi-national adopts a marketing strategy that has the effect of institutionalising minority racist attitudes on our streets.

Case Study 1:
Tennent's World Cup Advertising Campaign[7]

Now it is not for nothing that England is called the 'auld enemy' by Scots. The legacy of centuries of battles and social injustice inflicted on the Scots by English generals, and an enormous and enduring democratic deficit through Westminster rule, still creates an almost knee-jerk reaction against the English in certain contexts, usually at sports events, in Scotland. The historical facts: English peasants were kicked off their land and as badly treated as the Scots were by the English establishment for centuries; it was the Scots Lords, 'that parcel of rogues in a nation' to use Robert Burns's memorable phrase, who, in trying to recoup losses after the financially disastrous Darien Scheme,[8] did the deal to unite Scotland with England. However, these still do not cancel out an unjust history. English incomers have to be sensitive to this and understand that Scotland is a separate nation, with its own Parliament, legal and education systems, which is increasingly pointing to independence within Europe. Yet the commercial reality for Scots is that England is Scotland's biggest market for goods and services and for incoming tourists. History's legacy means this is not a relationship that can be taken for granted; it needs good will and kindliness on both sides.

This, therefore, is the context of a story that concerns anti-English racism in Scotland. Sometimes as a journalist you are forced to stand up and be counted and, as a result of this story, for the first time a leading Scottish company was forced to put a tangible commercial price on the sensibilities of Scotland's English ethnic minority and prevented from institutionalising anti-English racism in Scotland's city streets.

It began back in April 2002 just as World Cup fever was building in the UK. Press stories began to appear concerning Tennent's controversial World Cup ad campaign, designed to encourage Scots to cheer for the other countries in England's group: Sweden, Nigeria and Argentina. National flags with slogans 'Support Sven's' Team' (referring to the fact that England Manager Sven-Goran Eriksson is Swedish), 'C'mon the tartan Argie' and 'Och Aye Kanu' (referring to the Nigerian Arsenal striker). These ads were destined for ninety-nine huge billboards at stations, airports and main city centre sites in the four major Scottish cities: Glasgow, Edinburgh, Inverness and Aberdeen. The key selling message the campaign seemed designed to project was that macho Tennent's-drinking Scots would wave the flag for anyone but England during the World Cup tournament.

One could imagine what Scots, American or German visitors would have said had they been greeted with a similar campaign in England. However, Tennent's Communications Manager, happily hoarse from giving interviews, protested it was 'a bit of fun', in keeping with an established cultural norm. Scotland had not undergone the national soul-searching that the Lawrence inquiry had occasioned south of the border.

The *Daily Mail*'s Tim Luckhurst suggested that this was an advertising own goal,[9] unlikely to impress UEFA delegates considering the Scottish–Irish Euro 2008 bid and out of step with the good-heartedness of the vast majority of Scots. Yet Tennent's remained in denial. It insisted that this was only tapping into age-old rivalries, and that as the campaign was running only in Scotland, not England where Tennent's is not sold, this was deemed to be acceptable.

Now Tennent's is an imaginative and innovative company, which has led the way with cutting-edge and cheeky advertising for decades, and played a worthy part of Scotland's national life. But there is a difference between being cutting edge and cutting off your nose to spite your face. For it seemed to me that here was a classic example of a company failing to connect the obvious: that English families both live and work in Scotland and that English tourists would also drive past billboards while on holiday – perhaps not the 'welcome to the Highlands' they were looking for. And that though Tennent's is Scotland's premier pint, it is also just a wee brand in the big stable of Belgium-based global corporation Interbrew, along with UK designer favourites Stella Artois and Beck's.

The day after the *Daily Mail* article appeared, and on learning that in keeping with my long-held views on the damage anti-English racism does Scotland plc, I planned a column, more in sorrow than in anger, on this campaign. Tennent's seemed to panic, and offered a meeting with its ad agency, The Leith Agency, promising to pull the campaign if I could prove it was racist. Astonishingly, only then did Tennent's and The Leith Agency consult lawyers, although the brief had been assigned four months earlier, in January 2002. They learned that inciting racial hatred against ethnic groups, including the English, through published material, was subject to a police caution in Scotland, and a criminal arrestable offence in England and

Wales under the Public Order Act 1994. Parent company Interbrew UK's headquarters in Luton had confirmed that the campaign was to go ahead and so they were subject to English law.

Interbrew UK, obviously too busy sorting out its sale of Carling and the subsequent reorganisation of Bass and Tennent's, never replied to any of my e-mails or phone calls, in spite of its corporate responsibility mission statement on the company website, about following 'a right and proper path'.

Until then, it had apparently never struck Tennent's managers that, however much you love football, this portion of their £100,000 campaign was in effect, even if not in intention, fanning racist attitudes, seen in rising Le Pen-style racism across Europe. On the same day that I arrived at The Leith Agency, anti-fascist protesters were out demonstrating against Le Pen in Brussels, Interbrew's headquarters, following the initial voting in the French presidential election. I carried a strongly worded statement from the Commission for Racial Equality Scotland, confirming that 5 per cent of their caseload already concerned anti-English racism and calling on Tennent's to withdraw their campaign.

Tennent's Brand Controller naturally did not want Tennent's mixed up in an article about Le Pen. However, under pressure, she admitted that 'C'mon the Tartan Argie' might be offensive, given that an 'Argie' had broken the foot of David Beckham, England's captain. Nevertheless, the dominant emotion in the meeting seemed an abiding disingenuousness about a campaign that, very unusually, managed to have neither a working title nor a positioning statement.

The Times on 20 April had reported that the advertising campaign had been given the go-ahead by an English Marketing Director at Interbrew's HQ south of the border. The Leith Agency and Tennent's insisted that it had not – even though the artwork had been plastered over their notattheworldcup.com website for downloading by the media. Interestingly, the flags of countries playing in England's group were given, not all the others. The initial press reports had been leaked, they said, but not deliberately, unlike other campaigns. Most unbelievable of all, the billboards for the World Cup weeks had yet to be booked. More sinned against than sinning, they could be certain that whatever the fate of the English team in the World Cup, the brand had been established as the 'anyone but England', punter's choice for World Cup drinking.

To be fair, until I spelled out the realpolitik, I don't think they realised how dangerous to their own skins, as well as the brand, this ignorant, mean-spirited campaign really was. It was unacceptable, too, with a jumpy mainland European parent company operating in a climate of growing racism and anti-globalisation feeling, as well as the increasing pressure on companies to show joined-up thinking on corporate social responsibility. There were implications too, for Scotland's tourism industry, still recovering from the effects of foot-and-mouth disease, 9/11 and in competition for the first time with tourist destinations in the Euro zone. Scotland needed all the English tourists it could get. There were possible repercussions for inward investment and Anglo-Scottish relations. Tennent's, The Leith Agency and the World Cup could not be isolated from wider issues.

It was not 'a bit of fun', to experience, as I have, a bar in the Lothians, with regulars bawling against England, English tourists walking out, and English locals — high-flying professionals in Scotland's financial services community — sitting miserably wondering whether to open their mouth to order drinks and dreading what might face their children in primary-school playgrounds the next day.

Tennent's brand controller, to her credit, was appalled that there could be any such connections between Tennent's and small boys with English accents getting 'wedgied'. I explained the police Alport racism scale, based on studies of Nazi Germany, which ranges from 1 — racial abuse; 2 — exclusion; 3 — positive discrimination; 4 — violence. Racism always starts at 1 and works upwards. The race relations professional I had consulted felt that Tennent's were in danger of at least 1 and 2. All just to sell more beer.

I have facilitated race-awareness programmes with senior managers and it is dramatic when they finally realise they must change the story they tell themselves; in this case that 'it's just a bit of fun'. Until this point arrives, you can paper the office walls with race equality policies and corporate social responsibility mission statements and it makes not a jot of difference. The tipping point came with this story, when I revealed to The Leith Agency that I had rung a client to request their formal policy regarding suppliers who were open to accusations of inciting racial hatred. The client had told me that their company would seek to work with and dissuade the supplier from a practice that conflicted with its corporate responsibility ethos and values. If the supplier did not, then this would have a negative impact on the relationship.

This was The Leith Agency's leading client Standard Life, one of Scotland's most respected companies, a champion of corporate social responsibility with 80 per cent of business written outside Scotland. Only then did The Leith Agency senior managers look seriously discomfited, perhaps realising the potential of this 'bit of fun' to be more serious.

On the Thursday before publication, Tennent's rang to say it was issuing a statement and that it had decided to pull all the English group posters but 'Och Aye Kanu', with the rest replaced by artwork for the non-England groups, for example 'The Peebles Republic – of China'. Furthermore, the company would consult the Commission for Racial Equality on the rest of the campaign and it had taken my comments on board. Given its previous commitment, this meant I had proved the campaign was racist and that, on legal advice, they had withdrawn the worst offenders.

I wrote in *Scotland on Sunday* that this was a great result for Tennent's, and The Leith Agency, in keeping with their reputation for good corporate social responsibility. I thought Tennent's had shown genuine leadership, which would save the harmony of our civic life being chipped away just to make profits. I believed that Tennent's had set a tangible commercial price on the feelings on Scotland's English ethnic minority while sending a strong message to the rest of the marketing community. I also wrote that Scotland was too big-hearted for such mean-spiritedness and commercially we could no longer afford such disingenuous bravado.

I received the biggest postbag I have ever received for any story. All congratulated me except for two, which were so abusive that it rather proved my point about the depths Tennent's had been plumbing. The story was picked up by some of the trade papers, and it seemed a benchmark story. I thought that was the end of a nice good news story.

Sadly, I was wrong.

It was early June and the World Cup was in full swing – a cause of pride in Jubilee Year. Then I received an e-mail from a reader, a twenty-something English football fan who works near Edinburgh, who, after fruitlessly trying to obtain any response from The Leith Agency, Interbrew and Tennent's, sent me the letter he had written. 'Can anyone tell me why the flags are still up on Tennent's notattheworldcup.com website? OK, so they have been intermixed with non-inflammatory posters but the fact is that the flags were released into the public domain on an otherwise empty website with no explanation and free for all to download. Lots of Scots at my work did download them and now have them on their computers. Openly anti-English marketing not only being distributed by e-mail but on my colleagues' computer screens.'

I was amazed. Having pulled the offending ads off billboards and off the notattheworldcup.com website back in April, Tennent's had sneaked the original ads back online. Insidious, nasty, divisive and, being on their own website, conveniently not under the auspices of the Advertising Standards Authority.

Once I promised to take this up in my column, my reader speedily received an e-mail from The Leith Agency, admitting mistakes had been made. Yet the artwork still remained on the website. Tennent's managed an overfamiliar, irritated response, verging on the flippant: Tennent's had nothing to apologise for. It was all, once again, even after my first story, 'a bit of fun'.

But it transpired that Tennent's was only faithfully following the Interbrew line. When I rang Interbrew's Investor Relations department at the Brussels HQ, they had no knowledge of this little local difficulty, and politely thanked me for letting them know. Helpfully, they explained that Interbrew operates in twenty-six countries and that Tennent's merely follows one of Interbrew's nine marketing positions for local brands. Apparently, Croatia, Hungary, Belgium and Scotland follow the brand position that centres on male bonding. (Other countries, the tone implied, required a position of greater sophistication.)

So the harmony of Scotland's office life was apparently to be damaged for the sake of a Belgian multi-national doing it by numbers. Interbrew was less amused when I informed it that the Ethical Investment Research Service (Eiris) was considering featuring the story in *Corporate Ethics Overview*, its monthly fund managers' bulletin. Also, I had contacted senior managers at two international investment funds because they were currently researching the drinks sector in depth, and they were sufficiently concerned to ask me for any information I had. Both managers emphasised how very vulnerable a hands-off global player like Interbrew would be to reputational damage and a falling share price. Any negative campaigning in England, particularly if conducted on the internet, could be very damaging for it could purport to show just what the company that makes Stella Artois and Beck's really thinks of its customers.

Good business means understanding the big picture and not wilfully upsetting members of the public. I consulted a leading specialist in corporate social responsibility. 'It's a classic! Tennent's did not internalise the message of your original story, but merely thought they could manipulate themselves out of trouble.' He asked if I would mind if he used this as a case study in poor corporate social responsibility at a London conference next week before 300 corporate communications directors. And so the ripples of this little local difficulty were spreading.

By the following day the website material was removed. But the damage had been done. That morning a colleague took a call on *Scotland on Sunday's* business desk. The anonymous caller said he was the husband of an English manager working at one of Scotland's biggest insurance companies — ironically one that positions itself as a market leader in corporate social responsibility. He wanted me to know how upset his wife had been at work, surrounded by the Tennent's screensavers on colleagues' monitors. It was whipping up a vocal and negative atmosphere in the office against the English. There had been no support from the senior manager when his wife had raised this, and she had now lost trust in colleagues and confidence in the management. This hurried, whispered, anonymous call spoke of real corporate damage to motivation and productivity in the long term. However unmeasured and ignored, it was still damage to be accounted for.

On the evening of the day England played Brazil, an English friend in Scotland's central belt rang. His little boy had come home in tears, for that morning all the staff of his school, from the headteacher down, had come to work wearing green and yellow, Brazil's team colours. This had meant open season for name-calling, bullying and worse for the 20 per cent or so of English children in the school. It would be a long time before his child would get over it.

This particular school had taken part in national anti-bullying campaigns, and had equal opportunities statements on the office wall; but this gesture by staff was all part of a cultural disconnection. It was historic and understandable perhaps but, in today's climate, thoroughly unprofessional, damaging to young children and grossly offensive to some of the parents. The fact that there was no subsequent disciplinary action taken by the local education authority against the headteacher shows what a very long way there is to go. And what an opportunity there is now for business to take a lead.

The following week, standing on the stage of the Jubilee pop concert in Buckingham Palace Gardens, the compere referred to the Scots cheering for the opponents of the English team and asked the Scots to reciprocate as the English had happily cheered the Scots Ladies Curling team in the Olympics. This fact of Scottish life had, remarkably, not been common knowledge south of the border until the Tennent's campaign had received coverage by the London papers. Suddenly spelled out on TV by a sharp-tongued comic before a global TV audience with vast buying power, a Scottish senior manager told me later, this national blind spot appeared not just mean-spirited but commercially not very clever.

In the same month, Scotland and Ireland put in their £70 million joint bid to host the UEFA 2008 Championships. My colleagues on the sports desk told me that UEFA officials were easy to underestimate, that they always did their research and would know perfectly well about Tennent's 'little bit of fun', that a leading Scottish Football Association sponsor was promoting its products with controversial downloadable artwork, knocking the team of another UEFA member country.

Six months later, when the winning bid to host the European Cup in 2008 was announced, Scotland's bid not only failed but was apparently never even a serious contender, to the Scottish football establishment's mystification and fury. A successful UEFA bid would have delivered millions for Scotland's businesses. It is extremely unlikely that the bid was scuppered by a tiny part of a £100,000 advertising campaign but, behind closed doors, the issues uncovered in the Tennent's story may have added to the bid's other difficulties. And this, in a growing climate of racial tension in Europe, might have tipped the balance against the judges giving the bid any consideration. Who knows? In 2008, however, Interbrew will be making money, selling its local brands in Switzerland and Austria, complete with correctly numbered marketing positions.

November 2002
The WorkWorld Media Awards 2002, London

I am awarded runner-up for the title of UK Newspaper Feature Writer of the Year for making a difference to working life. It feels odd standing on a stage, being cheered by one's peers sitting at white-clothed tables. The story was a strain for my family and written at some risk, yet it seems a good example of how sometimes, when the disconnection between God and Money becomes too great, we have no choice but to stand up and be counted. For though the emotional pain and lost illusions of unthinking racism are never measured as deficits on any government or corporate balance sheet, nevertheless they impoverish productivity and community happiness.

The London sleeper crawled into Edinburgh's Waverley Station the following morning, past a billboard advertising the Scottish Executive's latest campaign. It said, 'One Scotland: Many Cultures.' Good news for everyone in Scotland.

Case Study 2:
The Musical Example of Fairway Forklifts Ltd[10]

Corporate social responsibility policies are usually associated in the minds of the public and the media with big business. Yet small, imaginative and cheap initiatives can have a disproportionately big effect in small- and medium-size businesses, which make up 97 per cent of the private sector. For example, staff morale and retention and recruitment issues have a far bigger effect on small businesses than big business. Margins are tight, so engaging with environmental concerns such as waste management can also save money, potentially the difference between survival and collapse in a downturn. Social reporting can also mean fishing in a wider pool for business, competing for tenders for larger businesses with social responsibility remits themselves. Best of all, it can deliver more sales through a higher profile and, with a happy staff, better customer service.

It was back in December 2000 when I first heard an extraordinary tale. A Glasgow forklift truck franchise had just appointed a composer in residence! This was no pre-Christmas fairy story; it was true. Karen McIver, one of Scotland's leading composers and pianists, much sought after by Scottish Ballet, Scottish Opera and leading orchestras, had been engaged to work for two months amid oil drums and exhaust fumes to find the inner creativity of forty mechanics and sales staff at Fairway Forklifts Ltd. Maybe this was a top-of-the-cycle story, but this I had to see! It turned out to be one of the most imaginative and long-lasting pieces of corporate social engagement that I have ever encountered.

So one Tuesday afternoon, I found myself on the windblown Hillington industrial estate near Glasgow Airport. Fairway Forklifts Ltd had just signed up to the New Partners Scheme run by Arts and Business Scotland (formerly ABSA Scotland), the UK-wide organisation which matches business sponsorship and engagement with the arts. Fairway, Scotland's largest independent forklift truck company, was then enjoying a 19 per cent share of a £50 million sector; turnover was £5.5 million. Karen McIver would work creatively with staff to produce a musical extravaganza to be performed for the company's tenth anniversary celebrations in May.

Frank Brown, the Managing Director, was direct. 'See, I'm not creative. I've just built up a successful business from scratch, but now I believe it's time for my team to get their eyes out of the mud and look up the way!' He explained that having given arts prizes and done up a community gallery with sponsorship in kind, he wanted a greater involvement in the arts in his workshops, which would also create opportunities for business growth. And now, for a tax-deductible £3,500, matched by Arts and Business, he had what he wanted. 'We always ask staff to think creatively, and to show initiative, but they have to be encouraged to get on that wavelength.'

Karen McIver, an immensely likeable and talented composer, decided to explore 1930s Bauhaus music with the staff, which emphasised the brutality of mechanics and industry. For added value, she would also write a musical logo and music for the company website.

It made a nice column. A few weeks later, I rang to check how the project progressed. Astonishingly, sales had already directly increased, because sales staff now had something to talk about to customers besides forklift truck specifications, making them more interesting to do business with. Fairway Forklifts was also increasingly positioned in the trade as an innovative company, which was further raising staff morale, productivity and sales. And the company profile had been hugely raised as the story had been written up in the local and regional press as well as trade journals, following on from my story in the *Scotland on Sunday* business section. Like all the best corporate social responsibility stories, this extraordinary tale was now operating on many levels.

Six months later, I returned to Fairway for their tenth anniversary celebrations. The workshop had been transformed with ruched tenting for the occasion and Frank Brown's £3,500 investment in good stewardship had seen productivity almost doubled. I was struck by the self-confident body language of the staff, who, through Karen's extraordinary music, had discovered new talents and abilities. 'Karen's music made us into a real family as a company,' said Frank. Suppliers, clients and staff mingled profitably. He proudly displayed special bottles of single malt ordered from Hungary, each with a glass forklift truck at the bottom. 'For the staff,' he told me, 'to show they're special.'

Clients were impressed, and some were now thinking about having an artist around the office themselves. Frank made a speech, the 1,000th forklift truck sold by Fairway was unveiled, and then the Show began.

It is always fascinating to see business people interact with artists. They usually exude a polite wariness as if they've turned up at a Tarts 'n' Vicars party by mistake. But the music soon stopped them talking. Sculptor Paul Marsden had constructed a professional art installation out of bits of forklift trucks, which was then subjected to a bravura performance by Karen and her colleagues, using forklift pistons and an oil drum. I turned to see this mainly male audience standing in wonderment. Frank Brown, the Managing Director, was beaming, completely happy. In the film which followed, staff – credited in a cast list – were seen typing in time with McIver's memorable Pathé News-style music, while 'Miss X', a dirty old forklift truck, was transformed by engineers Bob and Dougie, Fairway star mechanics, into a gleaming metal bobby-dazzler. Let me tell you, I now see forklift trucks in a whole new way.

The audience clapped and clapped. Of course, being cynical, you could say that these businesspeople had just cottoned on to the full power of Frank's brave artistic vision; that here was a nice wodge of matched public funding courtesy of Arts and Business and the Department of Trade and Industry, guaranteed to make any managing director look far-sighted and a boring product deeply sexy. But that would seem churlish. Corporate social responsibility is after all about enlightened self-interest. The best brand there is.

If there is a gap in the workplace between our values which are based on the love of God, and the way we do business, there is always damage to other people, always a bill to be paid by the wider community. Always a human cost somewhere out of sight, down the line. On the other hand, becoming a good steward is the most exciting job description we ever have.

8

HEY, BIG SPENDER! ETHICAL INVESTING, SHOPPING AND EATING

'The important thing is not to stop asking.'

Albert Einstein (1879–1955)

THIS chapter deals with micro money, the real money we spend either as investors and shoppers, very different from the big-picture subjects of the last two chapters. And yet the concept of stewardship, as a means of connecting God and Money, of putting us back in control of our lives so that we can make a difference, remains as pertinent as ever.

Ethical Investing

It is a muddy path up to the office, but the colours of the trees around are breathtaking. Piles of logs are to one side and it is only in the far distance, if I strain my ears, that I can hear the whine of traffic heading into Edinburgh. I should not have worn heels: they squelch in the mud.

'This is the sort of marginal company other banks probably wouldn't be interested in. But they're doing worthwhile work in alternative energy. Our job is not just to lend money but to give that extra layer of expertise to make the business a success.' I am spending the day with David Cousland, Loan

Manager for Scotland at the Triodos Bank (www.triodos.co.uk), the Bristol-based ethical bank which puts investors' money into ethical businesses, into alternative energy, sustainable housing and the so-called social economy, jargon for the not-for-profit companies and charities that make up a huge slice of the economy – £2 billion per annum in Scotland alone.[1]

The business we are visiting, a small sustainable timber company, is looking for £60,000. The talk becomes thick with woods and acreage and species of trees. David Cousland takes notes and figures and promises a speedy answer. Next stop, a computer recycling depot, part of a thriving not-for-profit group of companies based in an ex-mining community in Midlothian, employing young people who would otherwise be unemployed, and, finally, a business centre based in a former primary school. Triodos is hoping to pitch for the loan needed to expand into the church next door, so good is business. There are solar panels on the roof and big ideas in the management. I am impressed and wonder just how much private-sector business could learn from such enterprise and flexible thinking.

'About 25 per cent of our projects are eminently bankable with stiff high-street competition,' David Cousland explains. 'Half are bankable in mainstream terms but we offer added value in specialised sector knowledge, making us often the preferred lender. The other 25 per cent are marginal, but we would work to see how the project could fly and, because of the nature of Triodos, we often find innovative ways to support social businesses, which would otherwise struggle to attract finance.'

Every week the bank meets to discuss loan applications and each year publishes a list of its loan clients. In this way, savers can see exactly where the money goes; a transparency other banks could emulate. As a result, the bank is attracting large numbers of professional educated savers and investors who buy into the unapologetic ethical stance. Five hundred lenders and borrowers turned up for the bank's 2002 Annual Meeting in Bristol, where they laid on an organic buffet and seminars about fair trade, while the management set out their views of ethical investment, and won applause for keeping their own salaries at reasonable levels. Nirvana? Lala land? No, good business.

Hugely refreshing in an age when, as Alex McGillivray of the New Economics Foundation points out, 'lack of trust is found in all sectors, but few are as oblivious and obdurate as the financial services sector'.[2] No wonder this bank is putting on profits and market share as investors are given the double pay-off: interest on their money and the knowledge of where it is invested.

In the Parable of the Pounds in St Luke's Gospel (Luke 19:12–27), Jesus firmly places investment in a connected community context. And so, the good steward was rewarded responsibility for ten cities for his 1000 per cent return on the money his boss entrusted to him. The bad steward, who didn't like his boss and hid the money in the ground, is a passive aggressive business disaster and receives nothing. Jesus seems to make a distinction between investing actively in trading and enterprise, which is good for the community because it creates employment, and hoarding, which just means sitting on money unproductively. Reaping where we do not sow – lending out at interest, in other words – is usury. This is not healthy because we're not risking any loss of the money, and make no connection with the people it is lent out to.

Scotland's leading environmental campaigner, Alastair McIntosh, tells a good story of how he once calculated that if Judas Iscariot's thirty pieces of silver had been invested at a 5 per cent return per year for the last two thousand years, the cumulative interest if converted into money would weigh more than the entire weight of the earth. He tells me that he once actually did this calculation; his maths obviously is better than mine – I wouldn't even try. But tall story or not, it illustrates the uselessness of usury, the barrenness of hoarding.

Now it is very difficult to square this with our present reality where, if we are not embracing debt with both hands, we are always reaping where we do not sow. Unless we are the savers with the well-known ethical banks and building societies or investors in special share issues, which regenerate deprived neighbourhoods, most of us live our financial lives in a state of total disconnection.

Of course it could be argued that the most ethical way we can invest is to eliminate our debts as far as is humanly possible, and save up six months' money: neo-classical economists will tell us that, if everyone did this, it would bring down the artifice of the economic and financial system and lower living standards, an observation which in itself should stop and make us think. But the trouble is, even if we kept this money on deposit, do any of us have a clue what is being done with it overnight on the money markets, while we sleep? Of course not. Do we care? We don't think about it. We're asleep. And even if we try to find out, braving the finance company's hellish call centre with its multiple-choice question torture, it is doubtful we would get any sort of straight answer.

Stewardship, as I have said, gives control, but our financial system operates on obfuscation. With honourable exceptions, I tend to find that, at industry gatherings, transparency is considered rather a time-consuming pain, virtuous-sounding policy statements aside. Obfuscation underlines the 'don't worry your pretty head about it' attitude of the prowling market-economy wolves; obfuscation is threaded through the marketing material, known in the trade as 'the Guff'. Transparency inches forward, grudgingly, under the threat of regulation. But the onus is still on us to find out.

We must ask questions. For example, what is our bank up to? It is holding our money, so what is it doing in our name? And these questions should also extend to banks holding the money of organisations we work for as volunteers. Why not? We are giving our time and energy to raise money, so surely we should know what is being done with it? Questions don't take up much time, but their effects can cause rippling unease in any boardroom. In 2003, as Chairman of the Society of Authors in Scotland, I asked the Society to make its bankers, HSBC, justify their £9bn purchase of US company Household International, a moneylending business which in 2002 was fined $484m to settle allegations of predatory lending practices to America's poor in trailer parks. The new chief executive, Stephen Green, appointed in 2003 from the bank's investment arm on a seven-figure package, is an ordained Anglican minister and so I felt confident he would understand our concern – writers rarely being big-ticket winners in the market economy. My research on the web revealed concern among the fair-trade community that the bank intended to roll out Household International's business model across Europe. Now, it is time-consuming and troublesome to move bank accounts for an organisation, and banks know this; but they also need to know that if enough members ask questions without receiving proper answers, the bank account could walk, with collateral damage to their reputations.

Similarly, financial workers need to ask themselves questions about business practices that they are part of. There have been so many blatant and well-publicised cases of mis-selling by these institutions since the 1980s and many questionable practices, some of which are yet to emerge in the public domain; yet how many God-fearing Christians in sensible conservative employment in these institutions play an active role in these practices, lending them legitimacy, in between Sunday outings to the Church? These may be well-paid, comfortable jobs, which society values highly; but no one is forcing Christians to do them, especially when they are all too aware that they are flouting the principles they apparently hold dear. I can think of one or two major mis-selling scandals still to emerge.

I would suggest that this all-pervading disconnection between the money we invest and where the investment professionals put it is very convenient. For just as I have shown in other disconnections between God and Money – in the splitting-off of land as a resource for taxation by nineteenth-century economists who lumped land into capital; in the discrepancy between company policy and action; in the gap between markets and basic moral values in counting money; and in the chasm between indebtedness and freedom – it is always ordinary people without fail who pay the price. Equally it is always controlling vested interests whom this suits very nicely. Now Christians on the asset-rich side of the fence have often found the 'render unto Caesar' line a useful and profitable get-out clause for their consciences. But if the early years of this new millennium have a particular mood yet, it is emerging from the ordinary people, who are making connections between what institutions of our national life are doing and what they are costing the rest of us.

Few of us have the nerves, knowledge or funds for direct share buying; indeed, in the UK, the proportion of shares now owned directly has shrunk from 54 per cent in 1963 to just 16 per cent in 2000. We prefer to buy baskets of shares in investment products and leave the investment decisions to the professionals, but that does not mean there should be no stewardship in this process. Until now, perhaps, too many of us have assumed too readily that fund managers employed by the trustees know their stuff – when in fact, as we now see, they are preventive incantation practitioners to the manner born. Yes, even 'ethical' fund managers still have to deliver superior investment returns in competition with their main-stream colleagues. And given that most of us will never feel we have enough money, we assume our small stake is too embarrassingly puny to make a fuss about. Yet this is moonshine, for the history of ethical investment has shown what power lies in our hands.

It started in the nineteenth century, when Quakers and Methodist investors screened out companies involved in alcohol and gambling. Then, in the United States, in the twentieth century, growing grassroots activism led to America's huge Pax Fund, boycotting companies associated with the Vietnam War and South African apartheid. In the UK, Friends Provident launched the first ethical fund in 1984, and ethical investing has doubled almost every year. Tough ethical fashions have changed in this more secular age. Years ago, baddies were arms, alcohol and pornography, whereas now GM foods, unfair trade with the developing world and corporate governance top the list.

Ethical sector IFAs tell me that ethical investors don't have the plastic and mortgage debt burden of many mainstream investors, and therefore enjoy greater disposable income. *The Financial Times* reported that, post-September 11th, when investors panicked and either redeemed investments or stopped pension payments, one group of investors astounded City professionals by their resilience – ethical investors. This chutzpah comes perhaps from wanting to change the world as well as make profits, meaning we are seriously valuable customers.

Now this is not to say that ethical funds have not suffered big losses along with conventional funds since 1999. Ethical funds have been more in the firing line. This is because large chunks of the FTSE 250 Index are excluded from investment (such as alcohol, tobacco and defence stocks), while the weightless economy stocks (such as new technology stocks), which ethical funds tend to favour, can be extremely volatile. Yet, however depressing the short term, there is no doubt that the ethical sector is now not only accepted as a serious form of investment, but it has also pulled the mainstream sentiment into more pro-active investment, and in not much more than twenty years.

In 1989, when I was writing on the *Daily Express* personal finance pages, and first suggested writing about ethical investment, my editor jokingly told me to lie down in a darkened room. In those days, only £199 million were ethically invested in the UK, mainly belonging to churches and charities, written off as 'conscience corner'. The Body Shop with its ethical value system was considered distinctly dotty, all brown rice and sandals, to many City eyes. But now over fifty UK funds offer ethical investment, with between £3 billion and £4.5 billion a year under management; and, in spite of stock-market falls, is currently showing investor growth outstripping conventional funds.

Ethical funds have gradually merged into what is now known as SRI – socially responsible investment – which can be confusing. On the one hand, this is good: more pension money is screened for poor corporate governance, environmental reporting and so on, and there is far greater eagerness among fund managers to learn about reputational risk. However, on the other hand, when one fund manager estimated that eventually 80 per cent of the FTSE will be in SRI funds, the word 'greenwash' does spring to mind, a convenient watering down of ethical criteria which leaves lots of heavy industrial stocks available to invest in and reduces the need for the expensive research that ethical funds require.

Personally, too, I find it strange that companies who manage lots of conventional funds, with every vice under the sun, can keep a straight face while promoting their one ethical fund, which seems thrown in for the image. Other companies, however, such as Norwich Union, Jupiter and Hendersons – who won plaudits in early 2003 for bravely disinvesting from Shell in criticism of their Alaskan oil field work practices – are respected for their rigorous ethical investment practice. If you can find a good IFA that specialises in ethical funds, who can talk you through the possibilities, this is the best way forward. However, beware of funds trading on their goody-two-shoes Quaker past that have no Quakers on board at present.

So should we opt for an ethical fund or SRI? Ethical funds screen out the badness rather more – the mucky oil companies and arms manufacturers – while SRI funds prefer the cosier strategy of 'engagement-positive' investor relationships with goodies – perhaps alternative energy suppliers or socially responsible retailers. Of course, these can lead to giving too much benefit of the doubt; one Scotland-based fund, whose chief investment office manager I interviewed, gaily justified investing in Gap for engagement reasons, at the height of shareholder activism over allegations about sweatshop labour. It was only pressure from ethical IFAs and a negative press, including my own article, which caused disinvestment. Some

American SRI funds in the USA were reported to have held stocks in Enron, because of its local good works.

However, several useful milestones have helped to build up pressure. From July 2000, UK pension funds had to declare whether they followed a policy for socially responsible investment, leading to inevitable pressure on trustees from investors and, in July 2001, FTSE launched its FTSE4Good Index, bench-marking good corporate practice in environmental sustainability, stakeholder relations and human rights. There was much boardroom harrumphing when Tesco and Royal Bank of Scotland found they had been left off, while BP and Shell were included. Ethical investment professionals at that time warned against corporate window dressing that masked unchanged corporate behaviour. Unilever, for example, was on the index, though subject of an Ethical Consumer Research Association boycott for poor corporate governance. But the FTSE4Good Index has now established an ever-improving ethical norm. In March 2003, the Corporate Social Responsibility Index was launched by Business in the Community (see www.socialfunds.com). In its first year it assessed 122 volunteer FTSE companies, which has further contributed to a climate where triple line accounting, recording not just financial data but a company's impact on the environment and communities, is no longer woolly theory, but increasingly is seen both as best practice and a commercial necessity.

The biggest force for calling companies to account are the pension funds. In Britain, the occupational pension funds of ordinary working people are worth collectively around £870 billion – in fact the provider of capital for most business is now labour, us. This is why the TUC is campaigning for more trade unionists to be trustees, because they feel that the short-term drive for shareholder profits is being used against their members. At the moment roughly only 40–45 per cent of pension fund trustees vote at shareholder meetings of big companies, so more noise is needed. It does work. In May 2003, investor power finally came of age when shareholders

in GlaxoSmithKline voted down the chief executive's controversial pay deal. Just as well. Patrick Hosking, deputy City
editor of the *London Evening Standard*, rightly describes the
ultimate beneficiaries of pension funds and life policies as
acting like the most feckless of absentee landlords.[3] Companies
are now on notice and our pension funds can make a
difference.

The UK Social Investment Forum has led the way with events
and publications, slowly changing the climate, encouraging
companies to see the dangers of reputational risk and brand
damage. However, it is interesting that other UK bodies,
such as the AABA (Association of Accountancy and Business
Affairs), an independent group of accountants, economists
and politicians, are treading into new territory, challenging
the pick 'n' mix attitudes to corporate social responsibility of
so many companies and sending a wake-up call to investors.
They have devised a new measure of corporate accountability
that could eventually tackle global business or TNCs (trans-
national corporations) on taxation, and how much tax they
are, or more usually are not, paying in each territory. Guaranteed to make multi-nationals quail, it could yet force dis-
closure on just how much of their profits end up in tax
havens, leaving the communities where they operate to pick
up the tab. This is a true nitty-gritty bit of corporate social
responsibility, which could powerfully affect share prices and
investor sentiment.

If we have an occupational pension, we can ask for details
about its socially responsible investment (SRI) policy. The
public sector in the UK has led the way with over three-
quarters of local authority pension funds now employing SRI
screening. But if we find our own particular pension fund is
not on the side of the angels, we can make a noise. It makes
good business sense. The War on Want and Traidcraft Just
Pensions[4] campaign, conducted during 2001 and 2002,
surveyed 20 per cent of the pension funds and found a dire
lack of interest in transparency, with poor social, ethical and
environmental strategies. Just Pensions published a toolkit

to educate trustees and fund managers on the legal implications and the business case for socially responsible investment. Indeed, pension funds can be seriously exposed if
companies whose stock they hold suffer 'reputational' risk
because of bad publicity, such as Shell following the Brent
Spar disaster or Nike for sweatshop labour.

We can no longer afford to walk by on the other side. How
can we say we love our neighbour if we are not interested in
finding out whether our pensions are funding sweatshop child
labour or heavy pollution? It is a disconnection we simply
cannot afford.

Ethical Shopping – Where Grey is the New Black and White

As a financial journalist, there are few issues which give me a
greater sense of unease than sweatshop labour in the garments
industry. Obviously, it is difficult for companies to keep track
of every link in their supply chain, but that is not to let them
off the hook. Customers need to ask questions and show their
concerns, even if we can never know the true cost in human
misery of the clothes we wear. More than half the £25 billion
worth of clothes sold in the UK each year are imported, many
sourced from countries where labour laws are non-existent
or not enforced. In China, for example, collective bargaining
is effectively illegal.

Ethical Consumer magazine (see www.ethicalconsumer.org),
a godsend for anyone wanting to adopt an ethical lifestyle, ran
an in-depth report in 2002[5] on high-street clothing. Etam,
Littlewoods and H & M appeared to have no policy of providing
countries of origin on labels, while one branch of Marks &
Spencer, a key holding for many ethical funds and a member
of the Ethical Trading Initiative, threatened to forcibly remove
the writer of the report who was checking labels in a store to
find countries of origin. Her subsequent attempts to make
appointments and discuss countries of origin with the manager
were ignored. Just how many staff would M & S need if we all

started checking their labels and asking managers difficult questions?

It is about social justice and bad business. For sweatshop labour must be seen against the backdrop of hugely inflated executive pay increases in recent years. Remember, too, that while quality-control of garments in these third-world countries is exacting to the highest Western standards, somehow knowledge of the working conditions and quality of life of the workers who make them is waved away with SRI policy statements, or audits from big accountancy firms. You can only admire the terrier tenacity of the anti-sweatshop campaigns, who won't give up, however small their resources.

Of course these campaigners in the West are accused of over-emotionally imposing Western standards on developing countries' labour markets. For me, the key indicator is freedom of association for workers to negotiate with management themselves. If we think back to our old history lessons on those nineteenth-century struggles to establish the trades union movement in the UK, we can see similar struggles towards unionisation in the world today. We need to show our support for this by showing our concerns to the companies we invest in and buy from.

However little we have to spend, I believe we can all make a difference. It comes back to stewardship. Looking after our money as God's money whether we are investing or going out for the weekly shop.

Ethical Consumer magazine publishes annually *The Good Shopping Guide*,[9] packed with good information about making ethical choices when shopping. Did you know, for example, if you buy Bounty kitchen roll or Pringles crisps, makers Procter & Gamble have been subject to a boycott call since 1994 for use of animal testing? They were exposed in the magazine in 2001 for using an illegally engineered ingredient in Pringles crisps in India. *Ethical Consumer* surveys cover services too. I have always bought car and home insurance from Churchill Insurance, which offers great value and service, and very polite staff. Yet, until just before this book went to press, Churchill was owned by Crédit Suisse, which has subsidiaries in tax havens including the Cayman Islands – meaning more tax to be paid by their customers, that is you and me. In 2000, the company was found to be holding £400 million under false names in the accounts of two sons of the former Nigerian dictator Abacha. So what do I do? Let the company know my concerns? Definitely. Go to another insurer who would probably cost me more? Here I arrive at the real ethical nitty-gritty minefield made up of shades of grey.

It's not easy. We have to shop in the context of our own income. If we're broke and can only just about feed our family, then thank God for supermarkets' own brand. But even if our tea and coffee is virtuously fair trade and our back step crowded with bags of glass and newspapers to be recycled, we are still accessories to the fact of sweatshop labour and most other corporate ills, if we use most high-street chains or manufacturers.

So is there more than one way of shopping ethically? I think of a lady I once knew with impeccable Christian and fair-trade credentials, who thought nothing of parking illegally in a disabled car parking space at her busy local supermarket on a Saturday morning! So let us look at ethical consumption from another angle – by taking a long look at the weekly total of our consumption.

I write as someone who at the height of the late 1980s' boom once put seventeen binbags out for collection, so over-blown was my consumer lifestyle. I had a big overdraft and a rotten work–life balance and was having to service debt to keep my shopping habits. Something had to give. I chopped my Gold card and, since then, once a month I risk the title of neighbourhood bag lady by opening up all my binbags for an audit. On good weeks, particularly in the summer when I bring home produce from my allotment, I feel full of virtue – I also lose pounds in weight with so much digging. On a bad week, it's a horror story. How much packaging, how much unnecessary processed food has been used up with money I have had to go out and earn, and, what is more, pay tax on? Almost invariably the amount of rubbish reflects my weekly spending. And so, once more, I vow to be a more providential shopper, buying just what I need, even if it is difficult when working long hours.

Eccentric though this may sound, I find it occasionally useful, when I am feeling tempted, to visualise an item before buying it as a piece of rubbish in a binbag, or in a bag for a charity shop. This really brings home the futility of spending my money on yet more lifestyle goodies. Back in 1998,[10] I wrote a column on auditing the cost of rubbish and asked what would happen to the 30 million copies of Elton John's recycled version of 'Candle in the Wind' sold in aid of Diana Princess of Wales' Memorial Fund? Years on, I can just imagine the landfill they have required. As for the baby-boomer generation, what will happen when, like their Victorian ancestors who were likewise obsessed by property and possessions, all their houses are cleared and all that dated expensive lifestyle stuff chucked out? Even if much can be recycled, what is the point of having used up all that hard-earned money acquiring all these possessions? We can't take any of it with us, so what a waste of God's money and our energy – what mugs our possessions make of us, particularly as it has been our debt-driven spending that has been propping up the economy for years.

Now the idea of living providentially may sound boring and puritanical, but I rather think its time has come again. Perhaps this is the new creed which can take over the Protestant work ethic, the distortion of which has nearly killed us from over-work. For if we only use what we actually need, it cuts down enormously the amount of time we have to think about money, and the time we need to earn it. It is the antithesis of how neo-classical economists define economic activity, but, as I hope to have proved in this book, we owe them nothing. It embodies the principle of stewardship; it is hugely Green, ethical and, more to the point, gives us back financial control.

Back in the mid-1990s, I devised a one-day seminar in Edinburgh called 'Women Managing their Money'. Backed by

Scotland on Sunday and the late Scottish Amicable, the aim was to teach women to look at their financial life holistically, to stop them being hoodwinked by jargon and bullied by professionals. Though there were some first-class IFAs and pension experts on hand, the real stars were keynote speakers John and Irma Mustoe, then big on daytime television, who had just written *The Penny Pincher's Book*,[11] whose talk centred on back-to-basics stewardship: living thriftily. Many of the participants said they had little spare money to invest on their own behalf, but we sat amazed learning how we could turn penny savings into forty or fifty pounds a month with forward thinking.

According to the Mustoes, most of us have twenty-five or so spending categories we spend money on regularly, such as clothes, heating, food, transport and so on, which should be looked at individually, to see where savings can be made. Their best tip, which seems obvious common sense but I pass it on because it has saved me hundreds of pounds, is to wait four days before buying any big purchase. Almost always in the intervening period, I find out how to obtain it cheaper, or decide not to bother. The Mustoes believe that thrifty isn't the same as being mean; and it can mean saving lots each year, which can then be spent on holidays or investments. It is Micawber economics, cutting down slightly on expenditure so that income covers outgoings and money stops servicing overdrafts or credit cards, and starts giving life quality.

Their tips included: wiping shelves, breadbins, tiles and showers with white vinegar; storing soap bars in the airing cupboard to harden – soft soaps dissolve more quickly; using cereal bags for the freezer; egg yolk for hair conditioner; and keeping a record of every single penny you spend for one month – for a true-life horror story. All very useful. Personally, I drew the line at using wine corks as non-scratch scourers, turning old maps into lampshades, and sending postcards made of cut-down cereal-boxes; but I confess I have, in my more impecunious moments, used salt as weedkiller, and wrapped up birthday presents in old copies of *The Financial Times*.

Being this thrifty may sound eccentric in a booming consumer economy – we may feel life is too short; but, if it cuts down waste, the amount we have to shop and, as importantly, the amount of money we have to earn and pay tax on, why not? Somehow, their approach has a certain survivalist charm and seems a liberating antidote to the constant 'buy now' messages we are bombarded with daily, just because well-paid copywriters, sitting in some big-name advertising company somewhere, decide 'we're worth it'.

Which brings me to food.

Bread of Heaven, Feed Me Till I Want No More

The connection between money and food is long established. Even Shakespeare apparently knew that the more our spending is out of control, the more our weight balloons.

> *Lord Chief Justice*: Your means are very slender and your waste is great.

> *Falstaff*: I would it were otherwise; I would my means were greater and my waist slenderer. (*Henry IV*, Pt 2, 1:ii)

Shakespeare was no slouch in using this to splendid comic effect in one of his finest anti-heroes, Sir John Falstaff, that 'tun of man', 'huge hill of flesh', whose debauchery and high living allows Prince Hal to 'do normal' in the taverns of London before assuming kingly office. Falstaff, with his impressive girth, knocking back his bottle of 'sack' dry sherry, is Everyman. 'I am out of all compass' is his mock despairing cry, Tudorspeak for fat as butter and up to his eyeballs in debt. And so say all of us, particularly in January, when the newspapers are filled with dietary and financial make-overs. Falstaff 'lards the lean earth as he walks along', comments Prince Hall with delicious venom. But then the Prince of Wales, a pragmatic user of people, is thin, solvent and in control. In time, Falstaff is cast aside and he exits stage left. Unloved, fat and broke.

Money and calories are both units of energy, which reflect our self-control and self-esteem – or lack of it! An overblown lifestyle is soon seen on the scales, but if we fail to make this connection, others profit and we lose. In the UK, where personal debts are running at 110 per cent of household income, it is perhaps unsurprising that we consume the most junk food in Western Europe, with recent figures predicting that in the next twenty-five years three out of four adults will suffer obesity. This represents costs to all of us taxpayers. However, our lack of self-control is great for business; there will be lots of academic research grants, and supermarkets will no doubt remain the most profitable in the world, probably sporting a lucrative line in 'slimming' foods.

Curiously, in a secular age when so few people ever see the inside of church, religious language has been captured by the advertising copywriters. Thus ice cream and chocolate are celebrated for their 'sinful' allure. How devilish. And sexy. Heaven and guilt combined. Doesn't matter, just keep spending. Binge eating is followed by penitence. But as community ties weaken, as long as the Falstaffs of today can keep shopping, even if it leads to a truly gross Domestic Product, who cares?

So in order to wrest back control, we need to recognise that the overflowing kitchen swingbin is the dietary equivalent of those bank statements which thud through the door, the ones that require two hands to pick up, assuming our stomachs let us bend that far!

Breaking this cycle means stewardship. This is not my food, but God's. Now this may seem over the top, but, then, are our weight and spending making us happy? Stewardship is not a word seen on supermarket posters or in any newspaper, unless attached to part of a finance company wanting to sell us a pension. No one wants us to think about stewardship because, if we did, we would start thinking for ourselves. Stewardship in our modern world means grabbing back control for ourselves. In God's name.

Jesus tells us in Luke that the faithful and wise steward provides our 'allowance of food at the proper time' (Luke 12:42). If we think of that sentence it might help us resist the temptation of snacking in between meals on expensive, calorific, processed snacks filled with E numbers, made by some faceless multi-national – the wrapping of which ends up in landfill. Just thinking in these terms is very slimming and liberating.

Years ago, I was guest presenter on a programme called *Dosh*, a Channel 4 money programme with the late Adam Faith, not exactly a stranger himself to financial rollercoasters. I was sent to a council estate in Stockport, where residents had suffered for years from poor public transport, low incomes and very little access to fresh fruit and vegetables. Here, a group of mothers had banded together to organise a weekly delivery of fresh fruit and veg from a local greengrocer to the community hall. We filmed the weekly share-out, which soon had a party atmosphere. Business was booming, for the group had showed real marketing savvy, by devising a range of low-cost imaginative special offers to encourage new customers – for the bigger the order, the bigger the savings. For £1, a Pot Luck bag might include a cauliflower, a few grapes, some potatoes and carrots – whatever was cheap. Here was real abundance and financial self-control. Good food was replacing over-priced processed rubbish, which was eating up low incomes. It was inspiring to see how this group had unlocked the community's spending power and self-esteem, and was also helping a local business survive supermarket competition. Wise and faithful stewards like these are valuable people, not easily cast aside, or discounted by those in power, because they do count.

There are real political issues here. As Rachel Bowlby has observed in her book *Carried Away*,[12] overblown food consumption signals abandonment of social justice. Stuffing our faces unthinkingly blinds us to the hunger and poverty around us – not in Africa but in the housing estate down the road, where children may not have eaten a fresh banana for months.

Imagine for a moment Falstaff had stopped overeating and drinking, and started taking back control of both diet and finances. Not comic material for Shakespeare and the groundlings but, if it had happened in real life, Jack Falstaff would have been a far greater political challenge to the new Henry V: he would have been courted, not rejected. Life is more than food, as Jesus specifically tells us (Luke 12:23), but the way we eat is also a signal of how we see ourselves and our place in the world.

Welcome then to Just My Share Diet. I shall not be bringing out the book of the TV show, or the exercise video, but this diet does work, because it puts community back into the centre of our food-buying decisions, whatever our income level.

Good stewards operate in a community. Therefore, My Share becomes just that. Just My Share; no more, no less. It is the 'portion of food at the proper time'. Not My Share, which has to be greater than Your Share 'because I live in a better area, in a bigger house with more avenues of credit, so I deserve it'. Not My Share, which has to be more, because I am feeling depressed. Just my share. Just the amount that an ordinary person like me could expect to eat on an ordinary day.

The whole family can be brought into making the decision. Children love money and so, with patience, can be educated in stewardship, if this spending is put into a financial context of keeping more money in the family for trips out. So if we multiply the number of biscuits we might reasonably be expected to eat in a day by the number in the family by the number of days between shopping trips, we find that we will buy just three packets not six. Ditto everything else on the usual weekly shopping list. Why spend money buying more than we need? Retailers and manufacturers know that the more we buy, the more we eat, hence the generous two-for-one offers. These are not bargains, but scams. Wise up! They don't care if we waddle, we're just profit centres. Two for one could be more than Just Our Share: unless we can ration it effectively, walk on by. (Apart from anything else, it is such a give-away about the size of their normal profit margins – do they think we're stupid?)

There is a useful phrase in the City of London when it comes to buying or selling shares, which I find useful when shopping for food. 'Always leave something over for the next man.' This means never calling the top or bottom of the market, not trying to squeeze every drop of advantage when selling or buying shares, but always leave some profit over for someone else, otherwise you can get your fingers burned when the market tumbles or rises. Apply this to food, and it takes on a new context, with social justice factored into the weekly budget. These shares are just, bringing the community and the earth's resources into the product cost, leaving something over for the next person.

It is interesting to reread the tale of the loaves and fishes in Matthew 15:37, surely Jesus' ultimate catering miracle. The Gospel writer records that 'all ate and were filled; and they took up the broken pieces left over, seven baskets full'. The four thousand didn't eat until they were stuffed and throwing up, they just ate their share. No more, no less. They left some over for someone else.

Overeating in Jesus' world view was a sin, for it was evidence of hoarding without stewardship. Remember the rich man in the tale of Lazarus who, 'feasted sumptuously every day' (Luke 16:19)? What a slimeball! He gave no thought to his rightful share, his greed mirroring his gluttony. The man who thought he could build ever bigger barns for his stash was informed that he was soon to die and would have to leave it all behind. Jesus wants us to be free to love our neighbour as ourselves. Ergo, we must respect ourselves and our bodies. Try this diet and see what a positive effect it can have on our bank balance, bathroom scales and self-esteem.

For me, it was a wonderful cookbook published in 1989 which first put me on to the road to good food stewardship. *How to Feed your Family for £5 a Day*[13] was written by mother of four Bernardine Lawrence, when a failed business venture meant that her food bill had to shrink quickly from £150 a week to £5 a day. She began experimenting with cheap, wholesome recipes to save money and feed her family healthily; her book, though printed in the 1980s, should be reissued as a must-have for everyone with a family. Interestingly, the prices of ingredients she uses are lower today.

Quite apart from the delicious recipes for fish pie, home-made pizza and 'bargain' bread – did you know that an ounce of lentils has the same protein as an ounce of sirloin steak? – what is so extraordinary about the book is the sense of self-respect and self-control Bernardine experiences eating this way, even though she had never been so broke. Stewardship is not about how much we have, but how well we look after our resources, whether food or money.

Jesus tells us that life is more than food. 'Do not seek what you are to eat, what you are to drink, nor be of anxious mind' (Matthew 6:25). He knows that emotional insecurity makes us comfort eat, but do we feel any happier scoffing more than our share? Does Falstaff? Of course not. (Well, perhaps occasionally!) But the more we buy and eat, the fatter and emptier we feel, and the thinner our purses and sense of self.

So Just My Share eating puts community back into shopping. It was community that traditionally limited our share. In wartime, there was rationing. In peacetime, we used the local shops where, if we piled up the goodies in our basket in the corner shop, either we saw the 'weh-heh' body language of the shopkeeper, who thought Christmas was coming early, and felt foolish, or else there was some chat about why we were buying so much. Now there is more community in cyberspace than in our shops, and it is the poor and those on low incomes who suffer with high-fat and high-sugar processed food.

Recently, I met a marketing man who described the 'white noise' he imagines he hears in supermarkets. These are all the 'buy me' cries coming from the shelves filled with products which have been developed, marketed and sold by teams and teams of people with lifestyles to maintain – the boards of directors, the management, the workers, the advertising agencies, PR consultancies, design houses and market researchers. So many people involved in persuading us to buy because our work–life balance is so bad. He looked as if he needed a holiday.

$£$£$£$£$£$£$£$£

THE WEALTH OF SOCIAL CAPITAL – IF YOU'VE GOT IT, FLAUNT IT

'In a community of human beings working together, the well being of the community will be the greater, the less the individual claims for himself, the proceeds of his work he himself has done; i.e., the more of these proceeds he makes over to his fellow workers, the more his own requirements are satisfied, not out of his work done, but out of work done by others . . . suffering, poverty and want must of necessity arise, if this community is founded any way upon egoism.'

Rudolf Steiner, educationalist and
founder of the Waldorf Schools movement
Anthroposophy and The Social Question, 1906

I am being shown round our local Waldorf School, which is very different from the strict regimented school I attended. One teacher I speak to says that he has come from teaching at a conventional main-stream school. On his first day, he handed out some Mars Bars for a treat; he expected the children to grab them and run as they always did in his experience, but instead these Waldorf children fetched a knife and chopped up the chocolate for everyone in the playground to share. This was the Rudolf Steiner way. Throw in two foreign languages from six years of age and good academic exam results and it seemed to me that this level of emotional intelligence and teambuilding, far more than knowledge which is soon outdated, would be an asset beyond price in any future career the children might choose.

Emotional intelligence and teambuilding – yes, I admit these are jargon words from a career spent writing about business, but this episode perfectly describes the wealth this chapter is all about. Social capital. Defined by writer David Boyle[1] as the wealth we forget about when we are too busy thinking about money.

The trouble is that we do forget it all too easily. How can our wealth be anything but money? But while we try desperately for the numbers to add up, we may be quite splendidly and expensively missing the point.

For it is the way we count that influences our view of the world, and our abuse of its resources and our calculation of the potential of our fellow human beings. As we play this numbers game, we miss a vast source of wealth and potential lurking just under our noses which belongs to all of us. Social capital. It is the invisible power surrounding a shared Mars Bar that poor accountants can't count and therefore don't rate beyond the numbers of portions per bar. They can't see the point.

So who has social capital? And how can you accrue it or spend it? What *is* it actually, in real life? This depends on whom you ask. The term has a communist past, but is now generally defined as the sum of energy, expertise, experience, commitment, time (paid and unpaid), common sense, intuition and imagination built up through networks, which drive forward organisations, businesses and communities. Alternative economists tell us that it is networks of neighbours, friends and family, and the reciprocity of community ties, which add up to what makes life worth while.

Businesspeople say that social capital exists in the intangible exchange of knowledge that, unrecorded by conventional accounts, makes up so much of the wealth of today's knowledge businesses (such as advertising, PR and IT). Fortunes have been made by those attempting to conquer this new territory, with terms like 'emotional capital' and 'Buy-in benchmarks'. However, fashion is everything in the drive for the efficient corporate body beautiful, so fashion prevailed. We had 'total quality management' in the 1980s, and 'business process re-engineering' in the 1990s. Losses in social capital led to some extraordinary moves. In the late 1990s, for example, some slimmed-down companies reintroduced veteran managers as consultant storytellers, to tell 'fireside' stories about the company history to restore a sense of belonging. Microsoft. it is said, has just 6 per cent of material assets, meaning that the other 94 per cent is made up of intangibles – its expertise, creativity and so on. In other words, social capital, or something like it. No wonder Microsoft investors never get the full picture – let alone a dividend. For if we can't measure it, how do we know if we're paying too much, or too little? After all, it is not as if we really know what is going on with conventional numbers in the accounts, half the time.

The not-for-profit sector defines social capital as the glue that keeps society together, which, once unlocked, can tackle poverty radically by helping people help themselves, without the top–down patronage of charity. And as for the rest of us in our private lives? More on that later. But the good news is that we may have more wealth than we think, and we can flaunt this wealth with a clear conscience.

Yet if this invisible wealth is so precious, why, in an age of cyberreality, can it not be measured? It is principally because we are used to counting capital only as money, land and property in such a limited and historic manner. By historic, I mean fifteenth century. For the traditional method of double-entry book-keeping, invented by Luca Pacioli in 1494, merely recorded money in and money out. In a more spiritual age, the presence of God was taken as a given. Since then, however, as the secular has prevailed, everything else, God included, has come to be ignored, uncounted, not accountable, and unmanaged. God himself, therefore, has no place in business, as he can't be counted. He can't exist, because he does not add up.

Fraud prospers well in this black and white system, which imbues numbers on a page with authority and permanence, while vital company assets, such as knowledge, loyalty or calibre of staff, are ignored, or left off.

Hence, in this mad world, research and staff training development are put down as expenditure, the first to go when the going gets tough. People are a cost centre, downsized out whatever their contribution, to the point that some companies have realised that they had accidentally cut out the company soul. If one operated one's own family accounts like this, Granny and the children would be out on the streets.

'How much would it cost at market value to toilet train the MDs of the top 100 stockmarket companies?' An unappealing question once asked by *Future Shock* author Alvin Tofler, which best sums up just how much business needs the non-cash-based, social economy to thrive. What would the hedge funds[2] make of stocks of love, nurture, community trust, neighbourliness? The horrific cost of lost social capital becomes apparent to market-makers and policy-makers only when it has disappeared and we are presented with the bill for society's repair.

Yet there has not always been such blind reliance on number crunching. As David Boyle points out in his book, *The Tyranny of Numbers*, the legendary American accountant James Anyon advised his students to use figures as little as possible and use them only to express the facts.[3] What extraordinary common sense this seems post-Enron, when so many numbers were used to impoverish us.

Nationally, the state works out our place in the world with very limited data, which offers only a limited and skewed picture of reality. The term Gross Domestic Product (GDP) is the money value of all the goods and services produced in the country, while the Gross National Product (GNP) includes GDP plus income earned abroad. These measurements are not tablets of stone, handed down by Moses to the UK Treasury, but relatively recent terms, worked out in 1940 when the British government was forced to calculate how much money it needed to fight the war. They never thought to calculate the winning potential of our wartime spirit – the voluntary work, energy spent caring for others, or the green wealth which came from digging for victory in gardens and allotments. As for the energy of spivs during the war and afterwards, no government likes to count the black economy as wealth, though it is estimated to be worth between 12 and 14 per cent of GDP.

These limited figures encourage the worship of a limited god known as economic growth. Zero growth is terrible, goes the creed; good, steady growth will see us rise to a nirvana of prosperity. Yet what an unsustainable and wasteful society, this artificial economic growth delivers. So it is good for growth to chuck out and buy a new washing machine, but no good if we look after the same one for years. In this realpolitik, where is the room for human potential or creativity, or ingenuity, or thrift? Sir Charles Handy, whose books redefined business of the 1990s, suggests there should be two sets of national accounts: one which records mere money transactions and another set which contains all the other indicators of national life. Why do investment and expenditure count as the same? Why is education set down as a cost? What is that saying about how precious our citizens are to the state? And why not record wear and tear on infrastructure, as well as environmental and family breakdown as costs? Or voluntary work, creativity and family life as national assets? God knows, drug abuse, family breakdown, drugs and crime soon feed through as a cost to us all.

It will have to come, for this invisible wealth is huge. Everyone from the World Bank and think-tanks such as the cutting-edge New Economics Foundation, to social entre-preneurs such as George Soros, all consider social capital, unlocked by local programmes, as the way forward for future wealth creation and alleviating poverty in developing countries. Social capital may be unmeasurable itself, but it is spawning a huge new sector. In the EC alone there are 90,000 organi-sations working in the social economy, providing 7 per cent of employment (which is the same as agriculture). And yet the measure for social capital remains the Holy Grail for alter-native economists. One can see why, when poverty can be expressed in terms of free school meals or health and housing statistics, but there is no language to record the lost potential of a clever child from a deprived background who by the age of six is unlikely to catch up with an unintelligent middle-class child.

And what about us, ordinary people seeking to bridge the gap between God and Money? Assuming we have our own small stash of social capital, how can it heal the scars we bear on our back, from the batterings of the market economy? How can social capital give us back a feeling of control when our voices are not heard? How can we value this as part of our total wealth?

The discipline first of all is to see it as wealth, especially when we are worrying about money. In the early hours of the morning, tossing and turning, going over the balance sheet of our lives, we itemise money going out, money coming in, bills pending, expectations pending . . . We 'guestimate' what our house is worth within ten thousand quid just to stop ourselves going mad. Thoughts chase each other like rabbits across the night. So, instead of rolling over and going to sleep, let us look at our other balance sheet, at the wealth we ignore, because the market economy does not have the tools to define it as wealth.

Glasgow. On a wet Wednesday lunchtime. I am running a workshop entitled 'What Does Money Mean To You?' with an audience of men and women, employed, unemployed, self-employed, aged eighteen to eighty. We have already established that none of us feel we have enough money. Whatever our circumstances, naturally £10,000–£30,000 would make all the difference to our wealth and well-being.

I then ask them to consider their social capital, which I define as the non-financial parts of life which provide high value, quality and happiness. They have five minutes to consider all the different elements of their lives that yield this wealth. Here are the results below.

- good friends, family and neighbours
- good health
- the education we received from school, university or college
- use and enjoyment of the five senses
- our talent
- our specific achievements which have changed or helped others
- our social networks at work, home and outside (e.g. at the school gate or in the gym)
- communities of special interests (e.g. readers of a specialist magazine)
- local community and enjoyment of its history
- ability to communicate with others across cultures/being able to speak foreign languages
- stores of good memories
- feeling loved
- good books, music, theatre
- religious faith
- walking and appreciation of nature
- voluntary work
- our reputation
- cultivating an allotment or garden

Quite a list. Surely the most hardened number cruncher could not dismiss all this as unimportant, fluffy and intangible? Look at the list again. Most are either free or inexpensive, most do not consume precious resources. All make life worth while, all contribute to good health and happiness, all cut down crime and, as importantly in this dangerous world, contain the very elements which could help us to survive recession, war, homelessness and hunger. None are dependent on conventional economic cycles.

We could, therefore, argue that social capital is more valuable than money. It takes time to accrue but, unlike money, this capital does not disappear in a flicker on some Canary Wharf computer screen. True poverty would be living without any social capital, however much you had in the bank.

I ask the group to consider what proportion of their total wealth is their own store of social capital. Difficult working on two such different scales, but with imagination we manage. Answers ranged between 40 per cent and 80 per cent. So, I ask them, why do we not value such a percentage? We write down ways in which low social capital might increase financial outgoings, without reciprocal community ties. In a sense, this mimics an exercise much beloved by insurance companies, engaged in selling life assurance to cover wives and female partners, which puts a monetary value on the childcare, tutoring, housekeeping, gardening, chauffeuring, cooking and so on that the average homemaker does – showing that it totals hundreds of pounds each week.

My group decides that the biggest costs would be in services, in childcare, practical help during illness, and lost opportunities for work or leisure. These exercises reflect the importance of the shadow presence of social capital on a conventional balance sheet.

How crazy and impoverishing. This is why the conventional accounting accords greater value to a woman out at the office all day drawing a salary – she is, in the jargon, economically viable. The childcare, processed meals, services of a cleaner, gardener and so on that she buys in all add to economic growth. Whereas, if she stays at home, the energy and commitment she expends bringing up her child enriches no one, apparently, and adds nothing to the GDP. The numbers seem all wrong somehow, and we feel impoverished.

I suggest to my group that perhaps we might try calculating our social capital in the same way an accountant estimates good will, when valuing a business for sale or for inheritance tax. This invisible asset consists, literally, of the good will and customer loyalty built up over years by hard work and service, which in turn produces income. To measure good will for a conventional balance sheet, accountants deduct the cost of salaries and interest on capital and then multiply the averaged out so-called super profits by a number of years, depending on the business sector, usually between two and five years.

In this way, they can place a figure on an invisible asset as a percentage of the value of business.

We set to work. I ask them to deduct annual outgoings from their income after tax and then multiply the remainder by the number of their networks and hobbies, multiplied by the number of years they have lived in their local community, and all of this by the number of years on active reciprocal terms with their family.

For example, Jo Bloggs has £2,000 left over after out-goings from his £25,000 salary. He has two hobbies (supporting his local football team and French evening classes), two networks (his office and his child's school) and he has lived in the town ten years. Hence 2,000 × 2 × 2 × 10 = £80,000. Jo Bloggs is 35 years old, and has been on good terms with his family for all the past ten years: £80,000 × 10 = £800,000.

£800,000! Who wants to be a millionaire (in social capital)? It is worth adding that this figure does not put any capital value on other sources of social capital (such as good health, memories, music, friendship). Nor indeed of the enduring social capital remaining in communities long after we left.

Absurd, daft, crazy? Why not? It's only an exercise! But then funny money statistics are juggled all the time in Whitehall, and laid down daily at our expense to rule our lives – just think of the Mad Hatter statistics about land that I outlined in Chapter 5. Is it any crazier than conventional accountancy, which considers dead trees cut up for logs as having a value and contributing to the GDP, while living trees have no value at all? Exactly.

Anyway, it is good fun when participants suddenly realise that they are loaded. The most obvious effect, in a world where men continue to carve up so much financial capital, is a sudden, radical re-rating of female wealth. Many women are multi-millionaires in social capital. Billionaires? No problem. This huge wealth explains why women can survive bereavement, divorce and change so much better than men, and why older people, not least older women, have far more going for them than society realises.

If we accept that any disconnection between God and Money invariably benefits those with assets over those with merely labour to sell, we may perhaps explain why it is that men, who traditionally have held the levers of power in the conventional cash economy, have been able to do so much. And so little. For example, they have walked on the moon and invented the wheel, the internal combustion engine, the hedge fund and the dishwasher, as well as discovering penicillin and the DNA double helix, while apparently being incapable of devising any way of measuring social capital.

It is fascinating to see the new self-confidence in the body language of participants who earlier arrived announcing they were skint. They are now well-to-do individuals. One participant points out that when economies are booming, making money and consumption have greater value, but this trend is reversed in recession. People are nicer in recession because if they have not already stored up social capital, they have to work fast to catch up, and community matters more. 'I can now see that social capital is as good as money in the bank. Better in some ways.'

This capital has nothing whatsoever to do with economic growth and consumption but everything to do with a sustainable, happy future. Alan Durning, author of *How Much is Enough?*,[4] suggests that in the 1990s people were four and half times richer than their grandparents at the turn of the last century, but they weren't four and half times happier. Without taking a sentimental view of 'yesteryear' with its child mortality, hunger and poverty, even so, social capital was found in the poorest tenements, and it inspired political movements and changed lives. Wars, whether on the battlefield or in the boardroom, are never fought over social capital. The politicians and commanders don't think they need it. We know we do.

So mind the gap between God and Money. For we have two challenges. Yes, there is no widely accepted and effective measure to calculate social capital. Yet. And, yes, conventional numbers also do not add up – to our cost. We therefore suffer a double whammy. Government servants, heirs of the Victorians who were obsessed with counting and measuring, are obsessed with league tables and waiting times. Yet, today, public frustration with the public sector is also fraught with incomprehensible maths, such as 'double counting' (presenting the same figures more than once) and the arcane calculations behind Private Finance Initiatives, which mortgage future generations in our communities. Ordinary people are merely numbers, not individuals, to government. Like sheep, we cease to count as individuals, and the cohesion between government and the governed erodes, to all our peril.

The end result of social capital, so alternative economists say, is trust, which needs first to be noticed and then counted as an asset. Until this happens, we are all on a loser. The New Economics Foundation is already working on trust indicators for business, which if accepted, as its long push for social auditing has been, should really change the nature of annual reports and government spending plans. A Holy Grail, indeed. Consider how trust indicators would work on share prices, if they were itemised in those long share columns in *The Financial Times*, alongside the price over earnings ratio and the yield? What about voter and stock-market reaction to the quarterly figures of the NFGDP – the Non-financial Gross National Product. How it would transform the fabric of our national life; how rich it would make us as a country!

The trouble with measuring anything is that it defines and limits and crushes. I think of one young boy with learning difficulties, but full of ideas, love and special genius all of his own to inspire and care for others, who was defined by his local child psychologist as possessing an IQ which put him in the bottom 5 per cent of the population. That was that. This figure pigeonholed him forever into a neat no-hope category for administrative purposes, ignoring all other potential of the human brain, which could be expressed, if not measured, as spiritual intelligence, linguistic intelligence, emotional intelligence, musical intelligence and capacity for depth of thought. Measuring IQ is as limited and prescriptive as double book-keeping. It ignores love, friendship, community and human will, all the elements which confound predictions, and provide hope. What a sick joke of a measurement.

At the moment, uncounted or not, social capital remains our best defence against official number-crunching. Social capital does not add up; but that is the secret of its power, for its capacity for miracles is infinite. I found a parallel when attending a lecture given in Edinburgh by the senior engineer who had worked on straightening the Leaning Tower of Pisa. He explained to the audience that when he had originally fed the existing measurements and angle of the Tower into his computer, it fell down. Conventional measurements could not understand why the Tower was still standing after hundreds of years.

Social capital is our own magic tower which endures; it is the connection between God and Money, a fusion of the spiritual and the monetary, bound through Love, which is our biggest asset. Mind the gap? Perhaps we do not need to, if we learn to count this capital in the right way.

Case Study 1:
LETS – Social Capital as Local Spending Power

February 2003, East Lothian. I am spending an enjoyable Saturday afternoon at a local community hall. It is the Annual General Meeting and Trade Fair of the East Lothian Local Exchange Trading Scheme, which trades goods and services among 150 local members. I have been a member since December 1995, and it is an important part of my life – and my wealth too. As we start to trade, the standard of the baking, the artwork and the services on offer is extraordinarily high. I can feel my LETS chequebook burning a hole in my pocket. If you've got it, flaunt it! Someone is selling muffins, someone else handmade paper, others nutritional and marketing advice, weaving and pottery. Here Ellets, the local currency of the East Lothian Local Exchange Trading Scheme, rules OK. Not a name perhaps as exciting as St Andrew's Fifies, Stirling's Groats, or Manchester's Bobbins, but it works. And I'm feeling rich!

Welcome to the land of LETS – local exchange trading schemes – where 40,000 happy people across the UK, operating 450 schemes, use local currencies to access goods and services from their neighbours and local businesses. A new way of living and earning which is unlocking community vitality at £2 million per annum. All around me are people flashing their chequebooks, or arriving keen to find out how they can join.

This is real Christian economics in the twenty-first century, accepted as such even by people who never go inside a church. On my own table, besides outgrown children's clothes, home-baked bread and an advertisement for my next creative writing class, I am also selling copies of *The Cousins' Tale*, my second novel, in which Sarah, my heroine who bought the repossessed house at auction, moves to East Lothian and joins the local LETS scheme with its local currency, Lollops – to the haughty disbelief of her unfaithful husband, who works away in Washington at the World Bank.

For her, the local LETS scheme provides salvation and an extraordinary transformation, as she grows from doormat into dynamo. As for me, the author, in search of a plot, the LETS scheme created wonderful opportunities for comedy writing and is probably one of the best plot mechanisms ever devised for bringing characters together who would never normally meet, and to spark the story into life.

So what exactly is LETS and how does it work? The idea was first developed in British Columbia by academic David Weston and later developed in the 1980s by Michael Linton, who brought the idea to Britain in 1984 to the TOES meeting (The Other Economic Summit), which was an alternative answer to London's G7 summit. It was, however, the recession in the early 1990s that proved the springboard to UK success.

There is no issuing bank with LETS. It is a local currency issued by people, so it is always available and exists in purely notional terms, as a record of members' transactions. Each member has a chequebook, and receives regular statements but, importantly, balances are annually made public so everyone in the LETS community can see how much everyone else has invested in the community, in the volume they trade.

One LETS unit = £1. There is no interest charged on debits nor earned on credits. The fact that there is no interest is a huge plus. LetsLink UK, the central UK resource centre, estimates that on average 50 per cent of the price of everything we buy for cash is interest. Interest is simply one way of allocating charges for the use of money, whereas LETS is free.

Each LETS group publishes a directory of members' goods and services; regular social and trading events encourage trade. As it develops a parallel economy, it builds up the stock of trust and social capital. This is not barter because A might not want to do a direct swap with B, but would like to trade with C, who has an idea to sell to D. As the pool of skills, know-how and people increases, so it reaches a critical mass and members can ask themselves whether they can buy or supply in local currency before they do any transaction in the cash economy.

LETS reflects the wealth of local social capital, hence unlocking new spending power for those less active in the conventional economy, such as at-home mums with young children, the retired or unemployed. We earn even if we do a very small service, such as sitting in a fellow LETS member's home for a repair man. We are earning, and so we are economically viable. This does wonders for self-respect.

For me, moving to a new home in the country with small children and no extended family nearby, LETS meant an immediate and rich resource of help and support, as well as increased spending power. Looking back at my records, I see that in one month, for example, my printer was repaired by a fellow member for 30 Ellets, and two days later I sold an old guitar for 20 Ellets, a rug for 35 Ellets, and two copies of my latest novel at 12 Ellets each! The following week my website was updated, in part Ellet payment, which intrigued my publishers, our bathroom was repainted, and I bought two German lessons for my son. In return, I taught creative writing classes, ran a reading group and my husband took small groups to auctions.

When we moved house, we used the local removal firm which took part payment in LETS. Once again this economic activity was kept in the local community. LETS works well for local businesses, which can gain an edge over larger competitors by offering part LETS payment. For example, lawyers, accountants, architects, plumbers and local shops are all local members.

There is a huge diversity of skills on offer. I flick through the directory. Almost everything I would ever need besides basic shopping is here: childminding; start-up business advice; any art and craft you could imagine; bed and breakfast; lifts to the airport; plant, house and pet care; piano, swimming, golf and language tuition; household cleaning; car repairs;

and accountancy. From long experience of LETS trading, I estimate that even if the rate is officially one Ellet = £1 in terms of the 'social capital' that comes attached to the trade, the sum of its energy, expertise, time, ingenuity and neighbourly kindliness, we give and receive service at a factor x 4.

Local currency should not strike us as so strange, for it is just one of the multiplicity of currencies in our daily lives, which include smart cards, air miles, supermarket tokens and loyalty card bonus points, which can be redeemed for goods. Even in the most orthodox bits of Euroland, who would want to be reduced to just one single currency?

Notes and coins anyway now form only 3 per cent of transactions, while money itself is ever more represented by intangible processes with Bacs, direct debits and standing orders stealing in and out of our accounts, often in virtual purchases made online. The effect of this virtual money is a palpable sense of powerlessness, which perhaps explains our apathy as consumers, investors and voters. 'Buy-in', that buzz phrase, occurs most effectively within small local units, where the distance between the manager and the managed is smallest. And so it is with LETS, the community economy which empowers us at local level. We matter. Spending power without guilt: what a glorious feeling. This wealth is as valuable in its own parallel way as a home, or a car, or jewellery, or books, or a stamp collection, or Granny's silver teapot.

LETS spending unlocks vitality by ring-fencing the local economy. For even if we shop in our local high streets, our money is often sucked out of our communities and into the pockets of distant shareholders and multi-nationals. LETS also successfully reaches some of the poorest and most excluded members of society by being individual and diverse. In Leicester, the city council has launched Naari LETS, aimed at Asian women as a means of preventing isolation. Naari – from the Gujurati, meaning 'lady' – now has over 500 members trading Mofis. Bristol, Gloucester and Stirling use LETS to create allotments to bring fresh vegetables to low-income families. Some LETS schemes are glorified babysitting circles, others are large vibrant organisations with paid staff and sponsored offices. But the evidence is that if efforts are made to attract a cross-section of skills, they grow rapidly. Local dynamism can be seen on individual websites, such as trading sites offering Buzzards in Leighton Buzzard, Exes in Exeter and Bobbins in Manchester. Yet while this dynamism is local, the internet has given LETS a global reach; LETSLink UK the central UK office has received 50,000 enquiries since it opened in 1991 with members of the public keen to join local schemes or set them up themselves, while the Lets-linkup.com site operating from Australia allows LETS members to link up worldwide, from bread traders in San Francisco and the Tucson traders of Arizona to Ilasa Lets in Lagos.

Those who ask, 'Why not just use cash?' splendidly miss the point. Money divides; LETS brings together. It creates a reliable measure of value without inflation or currency instability. It is no murky part of the black economy either. All LETS schemes should be registered with the local tax office. Tax must be paid on professional activities for which we charge local currency. But we can also put down legitimate professional expenses in local currency. Activities or sales that are not part of your professional life are termed 'social favours'.

Sadly, however, with Benefits, unlike the UK Time Banks which trade in hours given or received, LETS earnings are regarded like all other earnings. More than 16 of hours LETS remunerated employment per week impacts on levels of Income Support and income-based Jobseeker's Allowance. But there is a growing lobby for change as LETS continues to demonstrate its success as a channel into which the jobless can move before working, and as a means of involving a growing ageing population in their communities. That there is any remaining official suspicion tells us much about the limitations of the state's economic calculations.

Case Study 2:
Social Capital in Business: The Power of Micro Credit[5]

I first spoke to Syed when I was writing for *Scotland on Sunday*. Actually this is not his real name, but he really does run a market stall in the 'barras' in Glasgow. If you have never been there, I recommend you go; it is both street theatre and great value shopping, but if you are on the vendors' side of the stalls, only the tough and committed survive. On Wednesdays and Thursdays, Syed, who is just nineteen, works the markets in Clydebank and Alloa. He sells T-shirts, men's jeans, polo shirts. His stock is usually thin because he can't afford to replace it. He has bank accounts with two major high-street banks but, when it comes to lending him money for more stock, they don't want to know, for he has no house to put up as collateral, and little track record. He only needs a thousand quid or so. If he goes to the money-lenders, they'll charge as much as 500 per cent. So he's stuck, along with 2 million other people in the UK who are owners of so-called micro businesses, trapped with low turnover and thwarted ambition.

Luckily for Syed, Street UK, the social business which offers micro credit to micro businesses, stepped in. Micro credit, real money which runs on the social capital of trust in 150 countries, among some of the poorest people in the world, has finally arrived in the UK after a twenty-year bull market, at last backed by government grants and withdrawal facilities from high-street banks. The brainchild of former Citicorp banker Rosalind Copisarow, Street UK lends up to £3,000 which is repaid within a short fixed period, after which borrowers like Syed can increase their loan by 50 per cent. Borrowers must have three guarantors. If they group-borrow, interest rates fall. Copisarow estimates it can take up to fifteen loans from Street UK before micro businesses begin to be interesting to the conventional banks. That's how far off the pace micro businesses can be.

The social capital, which somehow sticks such deals together in this less-than-perfect world, where accounts are iffy, and track records usually nil, delivers default rates which are currently less than 2 per cent, a level that conventional lenders would kill for. Street UK managers build trust by visiting the business, and looking at profitability, potential and cashflow rather than collateral, lending only what can be easily repaid once all personal and business costs are met. The application form is just one page long with an answer given within two weeks. Syed was lucky. He borrowed £1,000 in a group of four and is now making £200 per week more, after all expenses. He will have paid off the loan within eight months, after which he and his mates will apply for £2,000 to buy in Christmas stock. He tells me that his relations thought the arrangement was suspect at first, but it was no problem and that he had a rapid answer to his application. He appreciated how much interest Street UK took in his business.

Micro credit has been very successful outside the rich industrial West, in societies where family support systems continue to flourish. In Bangladesh, the Grameen Bank set up to provide tiny loans for women, mainly working in textiles, has unlocked huge social advances, not least freedom from political extremism. Rosalind Copisarow herself worked the magic before, in the 1990s in Poland, after the fall of the Berlin Wall. The Fundusz Mikro has issued 30,000 loans and now operates in over thirty-three cities.

What huge effects just a tiny amount of money can make. What high costs in crime and lost potential it saves the rest of us. Then why, in the West, is it so much harder to borrow small like this than, say, the megabucks which sloshed around the unknown dotcoms in the 1990s? Even though nine out of ten British businesses employ fewer than five workers, and such micro enterprises have generated more employment in the UK since 1979 than any other size of businesses, why do we not apparently value micro entrepreneurs?

Street UK now lends to 150 clients from Birmingham, east London and Newcastle. But the obstacles to expansion are huge and include boxy, unimaginative thinking of state agencies and departments, predatory money-lenders and banks that operate without a social agenda. It seems that the richer the country and the poorer the person, the less debt that person is able to risk taking on, for if he or she defaults there is no way out. Copisarow believes that it is this imbalance between wealth and poverty, combined with the fragmented social capital in the rich West, which proves such an obstacle for micro entrepreneurs to get a start. Yet, how much is our myopia costing us in lost potential?

This seems to be the result whenever potentially rich seams of social capital in the power of ordinary local people encounter the controlling centrist instincts of policy-makers and, increasingly, global business. They prefer quick, easily measurable results and clear black-and-white rules; their poverty of imagination is unable to comprehend that micro entrepreneurism initially needs more of a blind eye than a big stick in order to deliver down the line to the tax-paying grown-up economy.

Sometimes I wonder, when I talk to battling visionaries like Rosalind Copisarow, whether the efforts of ordinary people are valued by the politicians, the media and the financial institutions which dictate the national agenda. Let's face it, car mechanics, window cleaners, one-woman hairdressing businesses, plus the odd fairground trader cannot compete with the glamour of global business and our celebrity culture.

Politicians cannot boast about their sassy economic brilliance nor tabloid newspapers and City banks celebrate Syed's market turnover in T-shirts. As for economists operating in expensive glass office blocks, they are prone to spout conventional wisdom which says that micro finance cannot reach the poor, because they are too expensive to identify and motivate. So, how much better to spend taxpayers' money doling out charity than encourage others to go into business? It can almost be described as a quasi-feudal desire to keep the poor in their place. What are they frightened of?

Yet without social capital, which, like coral, takes years to form, the market economy cannot thrive. This is what companies who rushed into the former USSR countries discovered, when they found that the communist system had not left behind sufficient social cohesion to nurture private enterprise. Building social capital takes a myriad of small but vital personal victories, none dramatic or headline-grabbing, but infinitely precious nonetheless. If the high-fliers in the business community cannot count this as wealth, that is their poverty of vision, and it exacts a price on us all. It is usually only when the graffiti appears and the boarded-up shops send neighbourhood businesses down and out that the number-crunching accountants and statisticians realise too late that our social capital is exhausted.

The challenge facing individuals in this new century is to make our voices heard and our local wealth invested in our communities count. Whether our politicians, seduced by global business mores and neo-classical economics, will be up to listening remains to be seen. Big business, too, ignores us at its peril. But what a huge opportunity there is now for churches to prove their relevance to their communities, first in auditing and then in making use of their own vast wealth in social capital. This is wealth that does not reside in land, shares, buildings or silver altarware, but is invested within the church membership. Yet, because it cannot be counted, this social capital is too easily valued less than monthly convenants or correctly filled in Gift Aid forms.

We have seen just where our limited, money-driven thinking has got us in recent years. But now we don't need to accept that this way of viewing the world will always be in the ascendancy. Who is to say that the people in the world who know why they need to chop up Mars Bars for the common good won't have the last laugh? Why do we assume there will never be a means of measuring social capital? What changes there will be in the balance of power in the land when real, tangible, local community wealth is counted on a new bottom line.

10

CONCLUSION

JUST why did I write this book? This is often a question writers consider for, having lived with it for months, that first lunch we had with the publisher seems an age away. This book has been exciting to write, for it has covered an extraordinary time as the old millennium tipped over into the new. It has followed a market economy that swelled on greed and hype, growing bigger and bigger into a giant tsunami, only to tip over and crash on to the shore. What a challenge keeping up!

Riding high over the years at the very top of the water has been the business community – the technocrats, the financiers, the investment boutiques, the media barons and their lieutenants; landowners and the other asset-rich; plus those who service them, such as lawyers, accountants and chartered surveyors. Also pulled along were the pension fund managers and institutional investors, who were all swooshed up amid the bubbles, all thinking they were getting rich – and many of them were – beyond their wildest dreams. Then, in their wake, just beneath the top surface, came the excited middle classes, scooped up and revved up into fighting for resources, such as housing, good schools and lifestyle goodies. They also saw the market economy as the key to unprecedented easy wealth through housing price inflation, yet as the waters swirled about their heads, they could not understand why they also felt so powerless and so poverty stricken. It was the 'whine of '99', a prevailing mood of discontent that asked, 'If we're so rich, then why do we feel so poor, compared to our peers?'

Then there were those who had not been invited to the party. The public-sector workers, looking to have their efforts re-rated and rewarded, only to be disillusioned. Then, far from the sunlight, being dragged along the seabed, bruised and broken, have come the poor, the nearly poor and the homeless. These have seen no increasing wealth, but just a life enduring the rough disturbance from above, as the height between them and the top of the wave has grown ever higher. For there is no 'trickle down' from a tsunami, just a crushing weight.

A few think-tanks and media commentators from both the left and the right pointed out what was going on, but it was easy to be written off as Cassandras. It was only after the start of the new millennium, when the stock market had fallen by 50 per cent and boardroom standards were found to be so wanting, that people began to stand back and survey the damage. To quote that great Scots financial journalist Charles Mackay, writing of bubble economics in 1852, 'Men, it has been said, think in herds: it will be seen that they go mad in herds, while they only recover their senses slowly, and one by one.'[1] It is a lonely, slow and painful process recovering from such madness; I hope reading this book will help.

Both the financial press and the business community spoke of redemption in the months that followed. However, I felt they had not grasped the learning curve required. For redemption surely always has to wait until the last possible moment, to be meaningful and lasting.

In the Parable of the Prodigal Son in Luke 15, you will remember that the younger son takes away his share of his father's inheritance and squanders the lot in loose living. Then a famine hits the country where he is living and he ends up feeding pigs. He is so hungry that he envies the food they eat. Jesus says, 'he came to himself'. A nice line this, which the late William Barclay described as the greatest compliment sinning humanity has ever been paid.[2] Only then does the young man realise that he must return home, to be welcomed with open arms by his father and unenthusiastically by his mealy-mouthed elder brother.

If I were writing a column on this story, my first question would be, why on earth did it take the young man so long before he 'came to himself'? Why did he have to be envying pig swill before he realised that he needed God back in his financial life? Was it because he felt that the famine (i.e. market downturn) in his new adopted country would be soon over and then he would be able to climb back to the good life? Or because it was going to be so hard and depressing eating humble pie at home and he did not want to? Or was he just disconnected, depressed and in need of Prozac? What takes us so long before we can reconnect God to our own balance sheet? How low do we have to go? And this is answered in the story: down to pig-swill level.

So who was profiting from the young man's disconnection between God (his father) and his financial life, before he finally got the message? The list below follows all the archetypes I have identified in this book, who make money out of us when we don't allow our spiritual values to count.

Profiteers include:

1. The young man's fake friends, who enjoy the lifestyle he provides.

2. The retailers – tailors, brothel keepers, innkeepers, wine sellers, sellers of grand marque donkeys! Everyone providing the goods and lifestyle consumption he enjoys.

3. The elite controlling the economy of the country, who can only grow richer with the increased economic activity he generates.

4. The money-lenders who emerge once the money goes. As his credit lessens, so the interest rates inexorably rise.

5. The pig farmer who owns the land and the pigs.

6. The pigs that he feeds.

7. Finally his elder brother, who William Barclay suggests represents the Pharisees, the jobsworths who will one day inherit assets with the power attached. For me, he also represents the institutions in our society, that have a vested interest in the continued debt and powerlessness of ordinary people.

The only person who can break the young man's slavery is the father, who comes to meet him, puts shoes on his feet, a ring on his finger and his best robe on his back, signifying that he is a slave no more but a member of the family with power of attorney. Lucky boy. What Heaven, if there were just such a Father Christmas saviour for the rest of us!

There is. It is just our poverty of imagination that makes us carry on, until we are eating twenty-first-century pig swill, before we seek to reconnect God to our own unstable balance sheet. How much more do we have to take? Let's just cut to the bottom line and ask him to bring us home as his stewards.

It is not difficult for him. The father does not whine or reproach, he throws a party. No, it is only our ego getting in the way, the cause of all poverty and suffering. The good news is that the moment we reconnect our money to God, we regain such value! How much more we have to offer than the jobsworths who never put a foot wrong. For we have lived on life's rollercoaster, and have lots of worldly experience to bring to the party. It is surely no accident that Jesus follows this story with the tale of the bad steward, who reduces the money owed by his master's debtors in order to build up some social capital to see him through bad times of unemployment. 'For the sons of this world are wiser in their own generation than the sons of light,' comments Jesus (Luke 16:8). In other words, if only Christians could be as eager to be good, as the worldly are to obtain money and comfort, they would be better people. Imagine the Prodigal Son once he is back in the family business: there would be no stopping him. He would create huge value, lots of commercial success and really give that stuffy stay-at-home brother a run for his money!

Over the years, I have kept my newspaper columns in big portfolio books. I know one day they will be junked into a skip and it would be fascinating to know the financial story of whoever it is who will do it; perhaps writing this book will enable some of my thoughts about these extraordinary tsunami years to last a little longer. *The Times* columnist Libby Purves once said that the best a writer could hope for was that one day, in fifty years' time, his or her book would be picked up in a charity shop by someone who would find it a good read. Naturally, being human, I hope any reader who has reached this far will have paid the full cover price! But she is right. For one of the great frustrations of being mortal is that we never know what will happen next.

The luckiest reader of this book will be the one who picks this up in 2053 for ten euros at their local Red Cross shop, and can fill in what happened after the baby boomers. But if they want to know what will happen next, when they themselves have gone, then that's easy. Human nature never, ever changes, whatever the era, whatever the currency, culture or economic cycle. Our best chance of understanding this mad, dangerous, wonderful world, and the people who inhabit it, is to keep God onside for dear life, place him in the very centre of our lives, and follow the money.

$£$£$£$£$£$£$£$£

NOTES

Chapter 1   Introduction

1. James Buchan, *Frozen Desire* (Picador 1997), p. 38.

Chapter 2   The Childhood of Money

1. Dorothy Rowe, *The Real Meaning of Money* (HarperCollins, 1998).
2. Valerie Wilson, *The Secret Life of Money* (Allen & Unwin, 1999), see esp. ch. 11.
3. 'Money and Me' column, a series on sixty-five top Scottish high-fliers, *Scotland on Sunday* (June 1996–September 1997).
4. *Scotland on Sunday* (15 August 1997).
5. The Federal Reserve (the 'Fed'), the central bank of the United States, was founded by Congress in 1913 to provide the nation with a safer, more flexible and more stable monetary and financial system. Alan Greenspan is Chair until June 2004.
6. *The Love Child* (Hodder & Stoughton, 2000), p. 129; extract reprinted here with kind permission.
7. Keith Tondeur, *Your Money and Your Life* (Trinity, 1996).

Chapter 3   Debt: The Spiritual Danger of a Four-letter Word

1. *The Widow's Tale* (Gracewing, 1995); *The Cousins' Tale* (Hodder & Stoughton, 1998); *The Love Child* (Hodder & Stoughton, 2000).
2. Peter Ackroyd, *Dickens* (Sinclair Stevenson, 1990), p. 319.
3. London Business School/ABN Amro analysis, written by Professors Elroy Dimson and Paul Marsh.
4. R. H. Super, *Trollope in the Post Office* (University of Michigan Press, 1981).
5. *The Sunday Times* (26 March 2000).
6. www.antoniaswinson.co.uk.

7. Released February 2003 by Egg Bank plc/Dr Brendan Burchell Faculty of Social and Political Sciences, Cambridge University.
8. Henry Palmer with Pat Conaty *Profiting from Poverty: Why Debt is Big Business in Britain* (New Economics Foundation, 2003); see also www.neweconomics.org.
9. Adapted from Antonia Swinson's column in *Scotland on Sunday* (13 August 2000).
10. Credit Action, 6 Regent Terrace Cambridge CB2 1AA. Tel: 01223 324034 see also www.creditaction.com.
11. Church Action on Poverty, Central Buildings, Oldham Street, Manchester M1 1JT. Tel: 0161 236 9321.

Chapter 4 The High Price of a Lousy Work–Life Balance

1. Joslin Rowe: www.joslinrowe.com.
2. The Work Life Balance Trust: www.w-lb.org.
3. The Work Foundation: www.theworkfoundation.com.
4. A 12-point programme for Business to Combat Depression in the Workplace – Mental Health in the Workplace' (International Labour Office, 2001).
5. Fran Abrams, *Below the Breadline: Living on the Minimum Wage* (Profile Books, 2002), p. 1; reproduced with kind permission.
6. Samuel Smiles, *Self-Help* (orig. pub. 1859; IEA Health & Welfare Unit, 1996), p. 188.
7. Richard Donkin, *Blood, Sweat and Tears: The Evolution of Tears* (Texere, 2001).
8. Address to the people (New Lanark, 1 January 1816), quoted in Robert Owen, *A New View of Society and Other Writings* (Penguin, 1991), p. 120.
9. Smiles, *Self-Help*, p. 181.
10. Cadbury, quoted in Carol Kennedy, *The Merchant Princes* (Hutchinson, 2000 (pb; Business Pioneers), p. 40.
11. *Land for Housing: Current Practice and Future Options* (The Joseph Rowntree Foundation, March 2002).
12. *The Sunday Times 100 Best Companies to Work For*, ed. Alastair McCall (supplement in *The Sunday Times*, 21 March 2002); see also www.sunday-times.co.uk/100bestcompanies.
13. *The Financial Times* (20–21 September 2001).

Chapter 5 God Made the Land for the People

1. Archbishop Camaro, quoted in *Blackwell Companion to Philosophy: A Companion to Ethics* (Blackwells, 1990), p. 273.
2. Kevin Cahill, *Who Owns Britain* (Canongate, 2001).

3. Under the provisions of the Land Registration Act 2002 – in force from October 2003.

4. Cahill, *Who Owns Britain*, p. 5.

5. Andy Wightman, *Who Owns Scotland* (Canongate, 1997).

6. 'The Sorrows of Young Men', presented during Scottish Mental Health Week by Professor Stephen Platt, Edinburgh University, in *Scotland on Sunday* (15 October 2000). In 2000 there were 500 suicides of men aged between sixteen and forty-five: 34 per 100,000; cf. 16 per 100,000 in England.

7. For more on the Diggers, see Christopher Hill, *And the World Turned Upside Down* (Penguin, 1991).

8. Fred Harrison and Mason Gaffney, *The Corruption of Economics* (Shepheard-Walwyn, 1994).

9. Sir Kenneth Jupp, MC, 'The Covenant with God: The Jubilee and the Gospel to the Poor', in *Geophilus* (Autumn 2002).

10. E. M. Forster, *Howards End* (orig. pub. 1910; The Modern Library, Random House, 1999), p. 251; with acknowledgement to The Provost and Scholars of King's College, Cambridge, and the Society of Authors as the Literary Representatives of the E. M. Forster Estate.

11. The 5th Philippic was a public letter written in AD 43 in which Cicero criticised Mark Antony's military tactics and heaped praise on the young Octavian.

12. Detailed in Niall Ferguson, *The Cash Nexus* (Allen Lane, 2001), see esp. ch. 1.

13. Adam Smith, *The Wealth of Nations*, ed. Kathryn Sunderland (orig. pub. 1776; Oxford Paperbacks, 1998).

14. Henry George, *Progress and Poverty* (J. M. Dent & Son, 1976), p. 203.

15. Ron Banks, *Double Cross: Gordon Brown, the Treasury and the Hidden Cost of Taxes*, available from the Centre for Land Policy Studies. Tel: 0208 943 3352.

16. Professor Brian Short, *Land and Society in Edwardian Britain* (Cambridge History Studies, 1997).

17. Ibid., p. 336.

18. Harrison and Gaffney, *The Corruption of Economics*.

19. Ibid., p. 32.

20. Extract from Mary Rawson, 'Single Tax City', in *Geophilus* (Autumn 2002), p. 100.

21. Don Riley, *Taken for a Ride: Trains, Taxpayers and the Treasury* (Centre for Land Policy Studies, 2001). ISBN 1 90120 202 X.

22. Edinburgh-based E-Rail Group announced in October 2002 that it could raise the £25 million needed to restore the old south suburban railway purely from the rising value of rents on offices on adjoining land. In November 2002 New Edinburgh Ltd

announced it would contribute towards the £1.5 million cost of Edinburgh Park Station.
23. www.antoniaswinson.co.uk.
24. Scottish parliamentary debate reference: 30 January 2003 www.scottish.parliament.uk/official_report/session-03/sor 0130-02.htm#Col17593
Votes: for: 35; against: 13; abstentions: 59.
Motion agreed to: 'That the Parliament notes recent studies by the Scottish Executive and is interested in building on them by considering and investigating the contribution that land value taxation could make to the cultural, economic, environmental and democratic renaissance of Scotland.'

Chapter 6   Why the Markets Need God More than He Needs the Markets

1. Professor Andrew Oswald and Professor Andrew Clark of University of Warwick, 'A Simple Statistical Method for Measuring How Life Events Affect Happiness', in *International Journal of Epidemiology* (New Revision, January 2002).
2. *Daily Telegraph* (11 January 2002).
3. J. K. Galbraith, *The Great Crash of 1929* (André Deutsch, 1980), p. xiv.
4. Ibid., p. xvii.
5. As reported in *The Guardian* (27 December 2002).
6. A 'bear market' is when the stock market falls more than 20 per cent.
7. *Independent on Sunday* (22 December 2002).
8. Noble, quoted in Alex McGillivray, *What's Trust Worth?* (New Economics Foundation, 2002).
9. Kamran Mofid, *Globalisation and the Common Good* (Shepheard-Walwyn, 2002), p. 86.
10. Ibid., p. 90.

Chapter 7   Ethical Business – Putting God Where We Earn Our Money

1. Roger Crowe (ed.), *No Scruples* (Spiro Press, 2002), p. 53.
2. *New York Times* (13 September 1970).
3. Adam Smith, *The Theory of Moral Sentiments*, ed. D. D. Raphael and A. L. Macfie (Clarendon Press, 1976).
4. The Corporate Chaplains of America (www.inneractiveministries.org) currently work in companies employing as few as eight and as

many as 8,000 employees, and aim to have 1,000 full-time chaplains serving 1 million workers by 2012. In the UK the idea is still new, but in Cambridge a thriving ecumenical organisation called Chaplaincy to People at Work (www.cambridge-chaplaincy.org.uk) is breaking new ground.

5. David Grayson and Adrian Hodges, *Everybody's Business* (Dorling Kindersley, 2001).
6. Newbold, quoted in Crowe (ed.), *No Scruples*, p. 122.
7. *Scotland on Sunday* (28 April 2002; 2 June 2002).
8. In 1693, William Paterson set up a company to establish an entrepot on the Darien Isthmus (Panama) to command trade from two oceans. Scots put up £400,000 (about half of the national capital), and five years later the New Edinburgh colony was established. However, fever and English opposition forced the colony to be abandoned with the loss of 2,000 men and capital – over £200,000.
9. *Daily Mail* (22 April 2002).
10. *Scotland on Sunday* (7 January 2001; 6 May 2001).

Chapter 8   Hey, Big Spender! Ethical Investing, Shopping and Eating

1. Interview discussed in Antonia Swinson column in *Scotland on Sunday* (31 March 2002).
2. Alex McGillivray, *What's Trust Worth?* (New Economics Foundation, 2002); see also www.neweconomics.org.
3. *New Statesman* (27 January 2003).
4. Just Pensions, available from www.justpensions.org.
5. Ethical Consumer (June–July 2002), www.ethicalconsumer.org. Tel: 0161 226 2929.
6. *Scotland on Sunday* (7 January 2001).
7. www.maquilasolidarity.org/campaigns/Disney/report/htm
8. www.nlc.org (see also DisneySweatshops.org and www.behindthe label.org).
9. *The Good Shopping Guide* from *Ethical Consumer* magazine, available for £10 from Ethical Marketing Group. Tel: 0208 229 1894.
10. *Scotland on Sunday* (3 May 1998).
11. John and Irma Mustoe, *The Penny Pincher's Book* (Souvenir Press, 1995).
12. Rachel Bowlby, *Carried Away: The Invention of Modern Shopping* (Faber & Faber, 2000).
13. Bernadine Lawrence, *How to Feed your Family for £5 a Day* (Thorsons, 1989).

Chapter 9   The Wealth of Social Capital – If You've Got it, Flaunt it

1. David Boyle, *The Tyranny of Numbers* (Flamingo, 2001).
2. Hedge funds are funds that are able to trade in a wide range of financial products by using investors' money and borrowed money leveraged on this to trade in derivatives, taking advantage of small price differences in different markets. In fact, hedge funds are a misnomer, for they are less interested in hedging bets (i.e. managing risk) than in speculation.
3. Anyon, quoted in Boyle, *The Tyranny of Numbers*, p. 38.
4. Alan Durning, *How Much is Enough?* (W W. Norton, 2001).
5. *Scotland on Sunday* (6 July 2001).

Chapter 10   Conclusion

1. Charles Mackay, *Extraordinary Popular Delusions and the Madness of Crowds* (Wordsworth editions, 1995), p. xvi.
2. William Barclay, *The New Daily Study Bible: The Gospel of Luke* (Saint Andrew Press, 2001), p. 243.

$£$£$£$£$£$£$£$£

FURTHER READING

Debt

Selby, Peter, *Grace and Mortgage* (Darton, Longman & Todd, 1997)
Shakespeare, Rodney, and Peter Challen, *Seven Steps to Justice* (New European Publications, 2002)
Tondeur, Keith, *Your Money and Your Life* (Triangle, 1996)

Land Ownership and Land Value Taxation

Harrison, Fred, *The Power in the Land* (Shepheard-Walwyn, 1983)
Harrison, Fred, *The Pathology of Capitalism* (Shepheard-Walwyn, 2003)
McIntosh, Alastair, *Soil and Soul* (Aurum Press, 2000
Stewart, John, *Standing for Justice: A Biography of Andrew MacLaren MP* (Shepheard-Walwyn, 2001)

Corporate Social Responsibility

Hutton, Will, *The State We're In* (Vintage, 1996)
Hutton, Will, *The World We're In* (Little, Brown, 2002)
Klein, Naomi, *No Logo* (Flamingo, 2000)
Monbiot, George, *Captive State: The Corporate Take Over of Britain* (Pan, 2001)
Schlosser, Eric, *Fast Food Nation: What the All American Meal is Doing to the World* (Penguin Books, 2002)

The World of Work

Handy, Charles, *The Age of Unreason* (Random House Business Books, 1995)
Handy, Charles, *The Empty Raincoat* (Random House Business Books, 1995)
Handy, Charles, *The Hungry Spirit* (Arrow, 1998)

Kennedy, Carol, *The Merchant Princes* (Hutchinson, 2000)
Rose, Jonathan, *The Intellectual Life of the British Working Classes* (Yale University Press, 2001)
Simmons, John, *We, Me. Them & It: The Power of Words in Business* (Texere, 2000)

Understanding Markets

Bernstein, Peter L., *The Power of Gold* (John Wiley & Son, 2000)
Cohen, David, *Bears and Bulls* (Metro, 2000)
Fay, Stephen, *The Collapse of Baring* (Richard Cohen Books, 1996)
Frank, Thomas, *One Market under God* (Secker & Warburg, 2001)
Jay, Peter, *Road to Riches* (Weidenfeld & Nicolson, 2000)
Rawnsley, Judith, *Going for Broke: Nick Leeson and the Collapse of Barings Bank* (HarperCollins, 1995)
Rifkin, Jeremy, *The Age of Access* (Penguin, 2000)

Social Capital

Boyle, David, *Funny Money in Search of Alternative Cash* (Flamingo, 2000)
Henderson, Hazel, *Paradigms in Progress: Life Beyond Economics* (Berrett-Koehler, 1995)
Henderson, Hazel, *Building a Win-Win World: Life Beyond Global Economic Warfare* (Berrett-Koehler, 1996)

General

Brown, Callum G., *The Death of Christian Britain* (Routledge, 2001)
Gladwell, Malcolm, *The Tipping Point* (Little, Brown & Co., 2000)

Websites

www.antoniaswinson.co.uk (author's website)
www.cccs.co.uk (Consumer Credit Counselling Service)
www.corporatewatch.org.uk (Corporate Watch UK)
www.financevictims.co.uk (Finance Victims: for those in debt or who have been sold a bad financial product)
www.globaljusticemovement.net (The Global Justice Movement)
www.go.to/ccmj (Christian Council for Monetary Justice)
www.goodmoney.com (Directory for the Social Investor)
www.henrygeorgefoundation.org (Henry George Foundation UK)
www.jabe.org (Jewish Association of Business Ethics)
www.landpolicy.co.uk (Centre for Land Policy Studies)
www.letslinkuk.org (Letslink UK)

www.lets-link-up.com (LETS groups around the world guide to 1,500 LETS groups from more than thirty-four countries)

www.napf.co.uk (National Association of Pension Funds)

www.nicnet.org/bangladesh (National Labor Committee – see Disney page)

www.stewartshipforum.org (Stewardship Forum)

www.street-uk.com (Street UK)

0808 808400 – The National Debtline*

---

* National Helpline for debt advice.

$£$£$£$£$£$£$£$£

INDEX